Hello and welcome!

*Vor dir liegt der **Wordmaster**. Er hilft dir beim Wörterlernen.*

*Sobald du neue Wörter in der Schule besprochen hast, mach die **New words and phrases** in diesem Heft.*

*Die **fett gedruckten** deutschen Wörter sind Lernwörter. Sie fehlen im englischen Satz, damit du sie eintragen kannst.*

*Im Anschluss an die **New words and phrases** gibt es kurze Aufgaben, Rätsel und Wortspiele, mit denen du den neuen Wortschatz übst und festigst.*

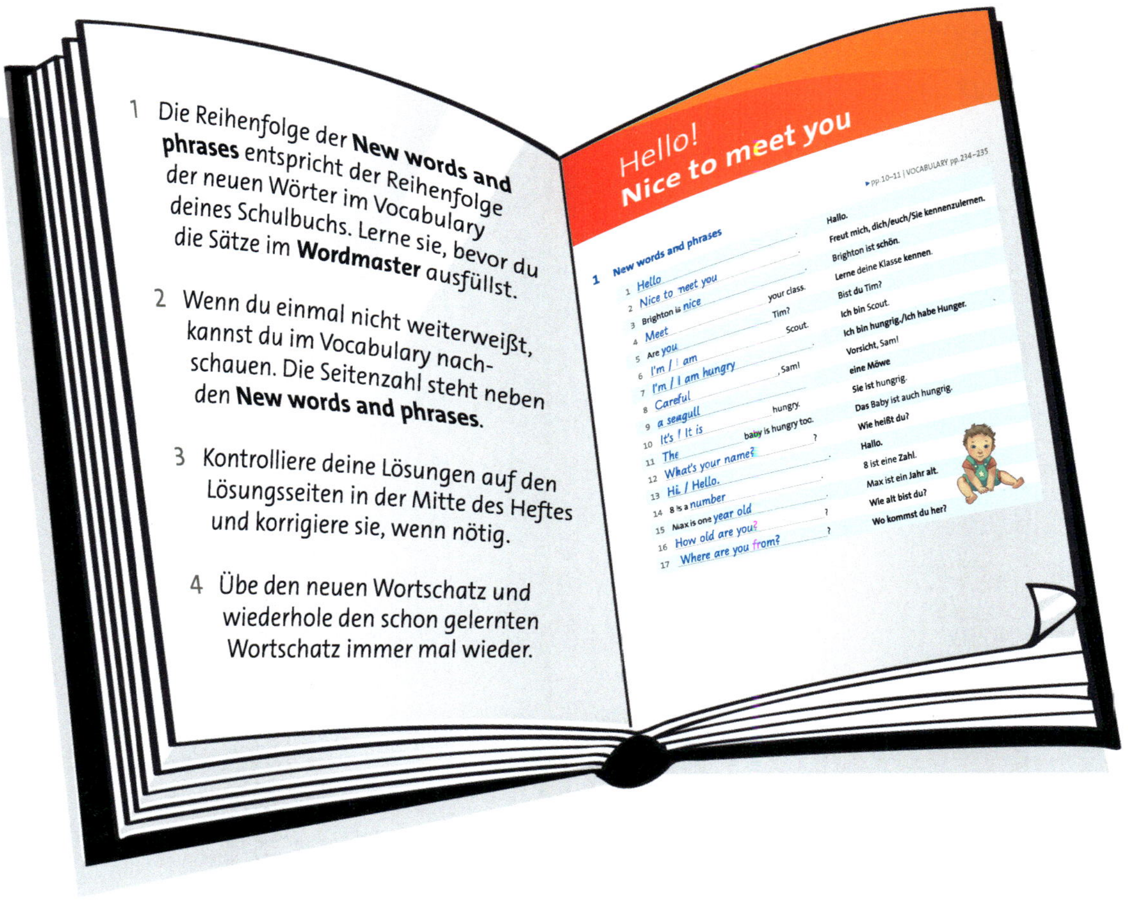

Alle Lösungen findest du auf den Lösungsseiten in der Mitte des Heftes. Die Hörtexte 🔊 zu den Listen carefully!-Aufgaben kannst du in deiner Cornelsen Lernen App aufrufen.

Hello!
Nice to meet you

1 New words and phrases

▸ pp. 10–11 | VOCABULARY pp. 234–235

1	______________________.	**Hallo.**
2	______________________.	**Freut mich, dich/euch/Sie kennenzulernen.**
3	Brighton is ______________________.	Brighton ist **schön**.
4	______________________ your class.	**Lerne** deine Klasse **kennen**.
5	Are ______________________ Tim?	Bist **du** Tim?
6	______________________ Scout.	**Ich bin** Scout.
7	______________________.	**Ich bin hungrig. / Ich habe Hunger.**
8	______________________, Sam!	**Vorsicht**, Sam!
9	______________________	**eine Möwe**
10	______________________ hungry.	**Sie ist** hungrig.
11	______________________ baby is hungry too.	**Das** Baby ist auch hungrig.
12	______________________?	**Wie heißt du?**
13	______________________.	**Hallo.**
14	8 is a ______________________.	8 ist eine **Zahl**.
15	Max is one ______________________.	Max ist ein **Jahr alt**.
16	______________________?	**Wie alt bist du?**
17	______________________?	**Wo kommst du her?**
18	Phil and Cal ______________________ seagulls.	Phil und Cal **mögen** Möwen.
19	I'm hungry. ______________________?	Ich bin hungrig. **Und du? / Was ist mit dir?**
20	Lisa and Mia like ______________________.	Lisa und Mia mögen **Fußball**.
21	______________________	**danke (schön)**
22	What ______________________ are seagulls?	Welche **Farbe** haben Möwen?
23	Seagulls are grey ______________________ white.	Möwen sind grau **und** weiß.
24	Brighton is in England – __________ or __________?	Brighton ist in England – **richtig** oder **falsch**?
25	I'm in ______________________ 5B.	Ich bin in **Klasse** 5B.
26	Hamburg is nice ______________________.	Hamburg ist **auch** schön.
27	______________________.	**Tschüs.**
28	______________________.	**Auf Wiedersehen.**

2 Colours

▸ p. 12 | VOCABULARY p. 235

Sieh dir die Farbkleckse an und schreibe neben jeden Klecks das englische Wort.

1  red

2  ______

3 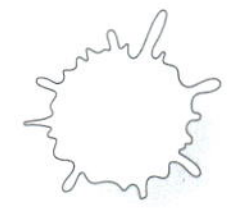 ______

4  ______

5  ______

6 ______

7  ______

8  ______

9  ______

10  ______

11  ______

3 Let's talk: Sich und andere vorstellen

▸ p. 225 and p. 227

Ergänze den Dialog so, dass er für dich stimmt.

Hello, I'm Sam. What's your name?	______! I'm ______.
	I'm 10. ______ are you?
I'm 9 years old. Nice to meet you.	Nice to ______.
	I'm from ______.
	Where ______?
I'm from Brighton. Bye.	______.

4 New words and phrases

▸ pp. 12–13 | VOCABULARY pp. 235–236

1	Tom and Amy are ______________.	Tom und Amy sind **im Urlaub**.
2	__________ and __________ are in the ______________ too.	**Mama** und **Papa** sind auch auf dem **Bild**.
3	______________ is hungry.	**Toms Mama** ist hungrig.
4	Sarah can see three ______________.	Sarah kann drei **Tiere** sehen.
5	four ______________ and two ______________	vier **Getränke** und zwei **Dinge zum Essen**
6	Amy and Tom like ______________.	Amy und Tom mögen **andere Dinge**.
7	______ is Scout. Tom ______________ Scout.	**Hier** ist Scout. Tom **kann** Scout **sehen**.
8	Amy ______________ Scout.	Amy **kann** Scout **nicht sehen**.
9	__________, __________ like footballs too!	**Denk daran, Hunde** mögen auch Fußbälle!
10	Hi, Tom. ______________?	Hallo, Tom. **Wie geht es dir?**
11	Thanks. ______________.	Danke. **Mir geht es gut.**
12	No, ______________ hungry.	Nein, **ich bin nicht** hungrig.
13	Hi Nick, how is Lucy? – She is not ______________.	Hallo Nick, wie geht es Lucy? – Es geht ihr nicht **so gut**.

5 Plurals

Sieh dir die Gegenstände und Tiere an und schreibe auf, wie viele es sind.

1 *two dogs*

2 ______________

3 ______________

4 ______________

6 New words and phrases

▸ p. 14 | VOCABULARY p. 236

1	______________________	**über mich/dich/Tom**
2	______________________ colour is blue.	**Meine Lieblings**farbe ist blau.
3	______________________ three Amys and four Bens in ______________ class.	**Es gibt** drei Amys und vier Bens in **meiner** Klasse.
4	Amy's ______________ is one year old.	Amys **Katze** ist ein Jahr alt.
5	Ben's favourite animal is ______________.	Bens Lieblingstier ist **ein Elefant**.
6	Luke's ______________ is nice.	Lukes **Pferd** ist schön.
7	There are ______________, ______________, ______________ and ______________ in Africa.	Es gibt **Löwen**, **Affen**, **Papageien** und **Schlangen** in Afrika.
8	Tom and Alfie like ______________.	Tom und Alfie mögen **Fische**.

7 Picture crossword: animals

Trage die richtigen Wörter in das Gitter ein.

1

2

3

4

5

6

7

8

9

10

8 New words and phrases

▸ p. 15 | VOCABULARY pp. 236–237

1	Ella's __________ is football.	Ellas **Hobby** ist Fußball.
2	Mara and Mina like __________.	Mara und Mina mögen **Sport**.
3	__________ your mum.	**Hör** deiner Mutter **zu**.
4	I like __________. What about you?	Ich mag **Musik**. Und du?
5	Leila can __________ nice animals.	Leila kann schöne Tiere **zeichnen**.
6	Abu's hobby is __________.	Abus Hobby ist **Tanzen**.
7	Jack can't __________.	Jack kann nicht **schwimmen**.
8	What's in the __________?	Was ist auf dem **Foto**?
9	Can we __________?	Können wir **Fotos machen**?
10	Tom and Amy __________ horses.	Tom und Amy **lieben** Pferde.
11	Aki and Dae __________ cats.	Aki und Dae **mögen keine** Katzen.
12	Zula and Lana play the __________.	Zula und Lana spielen **Gitarre**.
13	Nick's favourite thing: a __________.	Nicks Lieblingsgegenstand: ein **Fahrrad**.
14	Ari's new __________ is cool.	Aris neue **Kappe** ist cool.
15	Suna's __________ is big.	Sunas **Kette** ist groß.
16	There is a good __________ about snakes.	Es gibt ein gutes **Buch** über Schlangen.
17	Where is Lisa's __________?	Wo ist Lisas **Handy**?
18	Where is Jake's __________?	Wo ist Jakes **Roller**?
19	Sarah's house is __________.	Sarahs Haus ist **klein**.
20	Tim's bike is __________.	Tims Fahrrad ist **neu**.
21	Mona's house is __________.	Monas Haus ist **groß**.
22	__________ is Lara's chain. It's __________.	**Dies** ist Laras Kette. Sie ist **goldfarben**.
23	Jake's scooter is __________.	Jakes Roller ist **silber**.
24	You can play music __________ a guitar.	Du kannst **mit** einer Gitarre Musik machen.
25	Cats can't __________.	Katzen können nicht **lesen**.
26	__________ your guitar here.	**Leg** deine Gitarre hierher.

9 Listen carefully!

01

Höre dir die Sätze aufmerksam an und schreibe das fehlende Wort in die Lücke.

1 Please draw a grey ____________.
2 What colour is your ____________, Kim?
3 I can see a ____________.
4 Tim's ____________ is fourteen years old.
5 How old is your ____________?
6 Sarah can play the ____________.
7 Liu and Lin like ____________ and green.
8 What's your ____________ colour?

10 New words and phrases

▸ p. 16 | VOCABULARY p. 238

1 I like sport ____________ I don't like football.	Ich mag Sport, **aber** Fußball mag ich nicht.
2 The colour ____________ new scooter is red.	Die Farbe **meines** neuen Rollers ist rot.
3 You can put ____________ your books here.	Du kannst **alle** deine Bücher hierhin legen.
4 My favourite thing to ____________ is swim.	Was ich am liebsten **tue**, ist schwimmen.
5 Ruth's new ____________ is cool.	Ruths neuer **Hut** is cool.
6 Ruth's favourite hobby is ____________.	Ruths liebstes Hobby ist **Singen**.
7 This is my drink! – Oh, ____________.	Das ist mein Getränk! – Oh, **tut mir leid**.
8 ____________ your drink.	**Das da ist** dein Getränk.

11 New words and phrases

▸ p. 17 | VOCABULARY pp. 238–239

1 Sian, are you ____________?	Sian, bist du **bereit**?
2 The book is ____________ you.	Das Buch ist **für** dich.
3 Lucy's new ____________ is big.	Lucys neue **Schule** ist groß.
4 Jack ____________ be ____________.	Jack, **bitte** sei **leise**.
5 Lucy, please ____________.	Lucy, **steh** bitte **auf**.
6 Tim, you can ____________.	Tim, du kannst **dich hinsetzen**.
7 Rula, ____________ the ____________.	Rula, **schau an** die **Tafel**.
8 Please ____________ your books.	Bitte **schlagt** eure Bücher **auf**.
9 John, ____________, please.	John, **heb deine Hand**, bitte.
10 ____________ your books.	**Schließt** eure Bücher.

12 Listen carefully!

02

Höre dir die Sätze aufmerksam an und schreibe das fehlende Wort in die Lücke.

1 George, please put your ______________ in your rucksack.

2 Liza, are you ______________ for school?

3 ______________ is your hat?

4 ______________ to me, Liza.

5 Take your ______________.

6 Let's take a ______________.

7 ______________, there's a seagull!

8 ______________ your name?

13 Word search

Finde die fehlenden Wörter im Buchstabengitter.

1 Nice to ______________ you.

2 ______________ old are you?

3 I'm ______________.

4 I'm in ______________ 5A.

5 I like the colour ______________.

H	U	D	T	S	N
O	L	M	E	E	T
W	P	I	N	K	B
I	A	F	H	C	E
C	L	A	S	S	J

14 New at Park School

Sieh dir die Bilder an und schreibe auf, wie alt die Person ist und was ihre Lieblingsgegenstände oder ihre Hobbys sind.

1

2

3

1 Rula is *eleven*. Rula's hobbies are ______________

and ______________.

2 Dae-Hyun is ______________. Dae-Hyun's favourite things: ______________

______________.

3 Daniel is ______________. Daniel's hobbies are ______________.

15 Numbers

► pp. 10–11 | VOCABULARY p. 234

Rechne die Aufgaben und schreibe das Ergebnis auf. Schreibe die Zahlen aus.

1 1 + 3 = ____________________

2 5 − 2 = ____________________

3 9 + 5 = ____________________

4 10 − 2 = ____________________

5 4 + 3 = ____________________

6 2 + 3 = ____________________

7 1 + 1 = ____________________

8 12 − 2 = ____________________

9 5 − 4 = ____________________

16 Let's talk: Über Hobbys, Vorlieben und Abneigungen sprechen

► p. 226

Ergänze den Dialog so, dass er für dich stimmt.

Hello, I'm Sue. I'm new at this school.	
I'm in class 5A.	Hi! I'm ____________. I'm in class ______.
	What's your ____________________ sport?
I like football. What about you?	____________________
	____________________.
I like reading and drawing too.	
What about you?	____________________
	____________________.
That's nice. What's your favourite animal?	
I like fish. I don't like snakes.	____________________
	____________________.

Unit 1
My new school

1 New words and phrases

▸ pp. 18–19 | VOCABULARY p. 239

1	Sanya's hobby is ____________________.	Sanya mag Computer. Sanyas Hobby ist **Programmieren.**
2	Harper and Sarah ____________________ to school.	Harper und Sarah **gehen zu Fuß** zur Schule.
3	Liam and Ava love ____________________.	Liam und Ava **kochen** gern.
4	There are three new ____________________ in Pippa's class.	In Pippas Klasse sind drei neue **Schülerinnen**.
5	Tom is new ____________________ this school.	Tom ist neu **auf** dieser Schule.

2 New words and phrases

▸ p. 20 | VOCABULARY pp. 239–240

1	____________________ for a drink!	**Zeit** für ein Getränk!
2	Lucy is a ____________________.	Lucy is ein **Mädchen**.
3	Jake is a ____________________.	Jake ist ein **Junge**.
4	Lucy is Sophie's ____________________.	Lucy ist Sophies **Freundin**.
5	Jake and Kim ____________________ too.	Jake und Kim **sind** auch **Freunde**.
6	Mum and Dad are ____________________.	Mama und Papa sind **beschäftigt**.
7	Scooter the dog is ____________________.	Der Hund Scooter ist **müde**.
8	Mike's ____________________ is red and white.	Mikes **Krawatte** ist rot und weiß.
9	Mandy ____________________ dogs.	Mandy **hat Angst vor** Hunden.
10	Varndean School has a ____________________.	Die Varndean Schule hat eine **Schuluniform**.
11	Kim and Ruth are at ____________________ school.	Kim und Ruth sind auf **derselben** Schule.
12	"I'm ten years old." – "I ____________________."	„Ich bin zehn Jahre alt." – „Ich **weiß**."
13	Tom and Amy like ____________________ music.	Tom und Amy mögen **britische** Musik.
14	Joe and Alfie ____________________ a dog.	Joe und Alfie **haben** einen Hund.
15	Dunja and Carl ____________________ play tennis.	Dunja und Carl spielen **oft** Tennis.
16	Molly's new bike is ____________________.	Mollys neues Fahrrad ist **toll**.
17	This music is ____________________!	Diese Musik ist **schrecklich**!

3 New words and phrases

▸ p. 21 | VOCABULARY p. 240

Sieh dir die Bilder an und trage die richtigen Wörter in das Gitter ein.

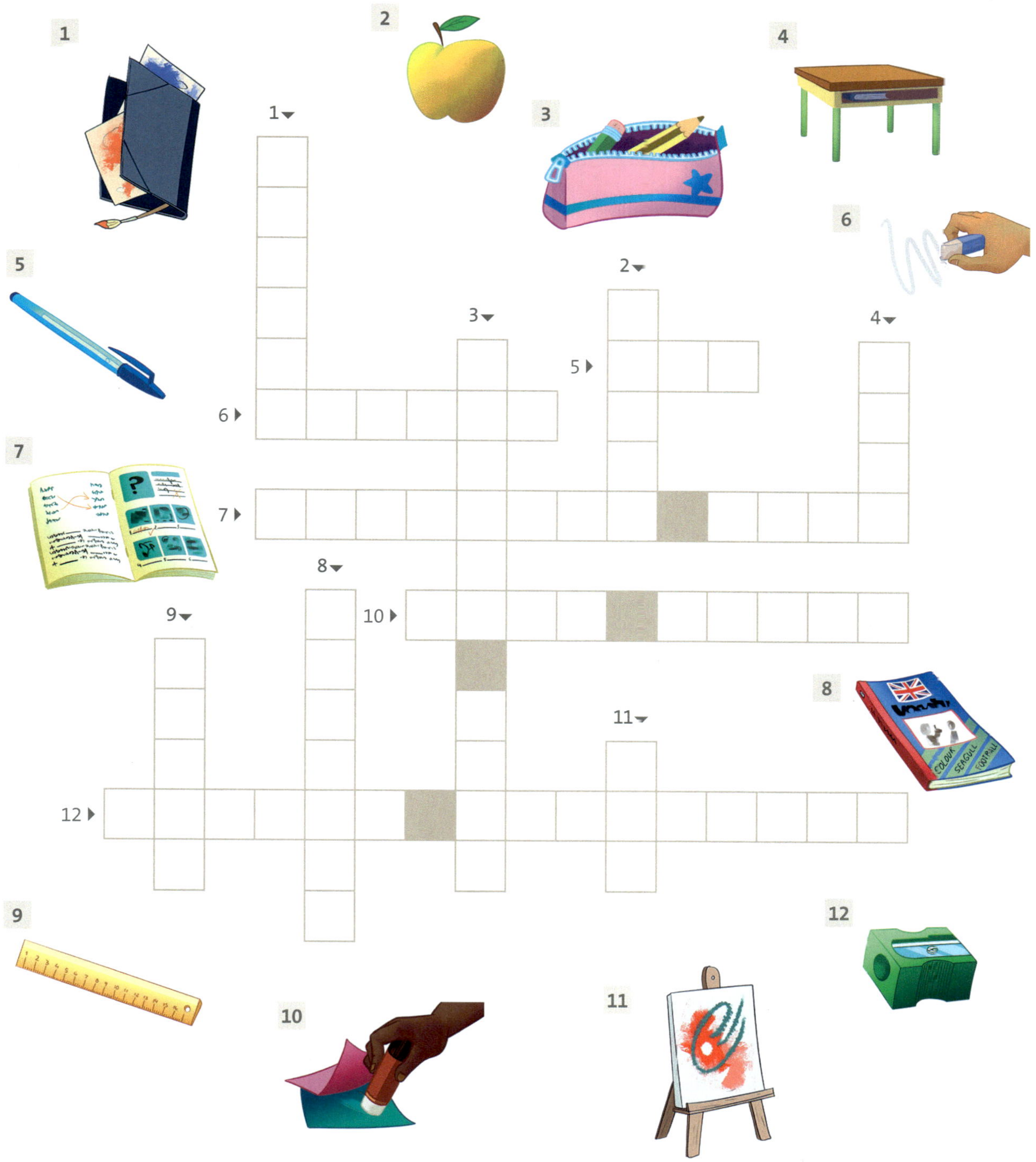

4 Odd word out

Unterstreiche das Wort, das nicht in die Reihe passt.

1 red – blue – photo – green
2 horse – lion – snake – drink
3 great – walk – read – cook
4 pen – apple – ruler – rubber
5 nice – good – great – horrible
6 seagull – guitar – monkey – parrot

5 New words and phrases

► p. 22 | VOCABULARY pp. 240–241

1	Tom and Ria have ______ hobbies.	Tom und Ria haben **verschiedene** Hobbys.
2	______ and ______ Black are Mum and Dad's friends.	**Herr** und **Frau** Black sind Mamas und Papas Freunde.
3	Tom has five different ______.	Tom hat fünf verschiedene **Lehrer**.
4	Sorry ______.	Entschuldigung, **ich habe mich verspätet**.
5	Tom, please ______.	Tom, bitte **verspäte dich nicht**.
6	Mr Brown is Liam's class teacher ______.	Mr Brown ist **wieder** Liams Klassenlehrer.
7	Open the ______, please.	Bitte öffne das **Fenster**.
8	"Are you hungry?" – "______, I am."	„Bist du hungrig?" – „**Ja,** bin ich."
9	"Mr Kelly is my new English teacher." – "Oh ______! He is horrible."	„Mr Kelly ist mein neuer Englischlehrer" – „Oh **nein**, der ist schrecklich!"
10	We often ______ to London.	Wir **fahren** oft nach London.
11	I walk ______ school.	Ich gehe zu Fuß **zur** Schule.
12	Where is the ______?	Wo ist die **Toilette**?
13	You can take photos ______.	Du kannst **jetzt** Fotos machen.
14	I ______ my rucksack to school.	Ich **nehme** meinen Rucksack **mit** zur Schule.
15	Can you ______ that again, please?	Könntest du das bitte noch einmal **sagen**?
16	Can we ______ about my party now?	Können wir jetzt über meine Party **sprechen**?
17	______ eat now.	**Lasst uns** jetzt essen.
18	Sing with ______!	Sing mit **uns**!
19	______ with number 1.	**Fang** mit Nummer 1 **an**.
20	Evie is at a ______ ______ now.	Evie ist jetzt auf einer **weiterführenden Schule**.

6 New words and phrases

▸ p. 23 | VOCABULARY pp. 241–242

1	Listen to your teacher ____________.	Höre **im Unterricht** deinem Lehrer zu!
2	____________ is it?	**Welche Seite** ist das?
3	It's on ____________ 3.	Es ist auf **Seite** 3.
4	Sorry, I don't ____________ you.	Entschuldigung, ich **verstehe** Sie nicht.
5	Can I ____________ you?	Kann ich Ihnen **helfen**?
6	I don't understand the ____________.	Ich verstehe die **Frage** nicht.
7	The ____________ ____________ is "yes".	Die **Antwort auf deine Frage** ist „ja".
8	"Can I ____________ your ruler?" –	„Kann ich dein Lineal **benutzen**?" –
9	"Yes, ____________."	„Ja, **bitte schön**."
10	"Thanks." – "____________."	„Danke." – **„Bitte, gern geschehen."**
11	"Where is Liz?" – "____________ Mum."	„Wo ist Liz?" – „**Frag** Mama."
12	Ria's new ____________ is big.	Rias neues **Klassenzimmer** ist groß.

7 Lost words

Vervollständige die Sätze mit dem richtigen Wort.

draw • go • open • play • start • use

1 Let's ____________ now.
2 Please ____________ an elephant.
3 Can you ____________ the guitar?
4 Please ____________ with exercise 1.
5 Can I ____________ your rubber?
6 Please ____________ the window.

8 Word snake

Finde sechs Wörter in der Schlange und setze sie in die richtigen Lücken ein.

1 Ye-jun and Marnie are in the ____________ class.
2 Marnie is Ye-jun's ____________.
3 Ye-jun and Marnie love ____________.
4 They ____________ read books about it.
5 They like Ms Reed, the English ____________ too.
6 Marnie has a nice ____________ case.

9 New words and phrases

► p. 24 | VOCABULARY pp. 242–243

1	This is Ella's ______________.	Das ist Ellas **Stundenplan**.
2	Ella's first ______________ is English.	Ellas erste **Stunde** ist Englisch.
3	Ella and Liam are ten. ______________ friends.	Ella und Liam sind zehn. **Sie sind** Freunde.
4	______________ in the same class.	**Sie sind nicht** in derselben Klasse.
5	Sorry, where is ______________ 105?	Entschuldigung, wo ist **Raum** 105?
6	Be quiet, please. The baby ______________.	Sei bitte leise. Das Baby **schläft**.
7	This is Sian. ______________ ten years old.	Das ist Sian. **Er ist** zehn Jahre alt.
8	Where is Liam? ______________ at school.	Wo ist Liam? **Er ist nicht** in der Schule.
9	______________ he is late.	**Ich glaube**, er verspätet sich.
10	______________, Liz, the cat is hungry.	**Du hast Recht**, Liz, die Katze ist hungrig.
11	This is Ms Cox. ______________ Kim's mum.	Das ist Frau Cox. **Sie ist** Kims Mama.
12	______________ friends.	**Wir sind** Freunde.
13	Students like ______________.	Schülerinnen und Schüler mögen **Pausen**.
14	It's time for the English lesson ______________.	Es ist **bald** Zeit für die Englischstunde.
15	Lessons at Kim's school are 45 ______________.	Unterrichtsstunden an Kims Schule dauern 45 **Minuten**.
16	There are five ______________ in the photo.	Auf dem Foto sind fünf **Leute**.

10 Letter code

Welche Buchstaben sind 1, 2, 3 und 4?

1 1 2e Englis2 less3ns a4e in 4 3 3m 6.

2 W2a1's 1 2e answe4 1 3 ques1i3 n 5?

3 F3u4 s1uden1s a4e 1i4ed.

4 B4eak is in 1en minu1es.

1:

2:

3:

4:

11 New words and phrases

► p. 25 | VOCABULARY pp. 243–244

1 I have a new ____________ on my phone. It's from my mum.	Ich habe eine neue **Nachricht** auf meinem Handy. Sie ist von meiner Mama.
2 Ron and Julia ____________. They have a big house, two dogs and a horse.	Ron und Julia **haben Glück**. Sie haben ein großes Haus, zwei Hunde und ein Pferd.
3 "Bye, John." – "____________."	„Tschüs, John." – **„Bis dann."**
4 ____________ Ms Cox, I like your art lessons.	**Liebe** Frau Cox, ich mag Ihre Kunststunden.
5 Art ____________.	Kunstunterricht **macht Spaß**.
6 ____________, Dylan	**Ihr** Dylan
7 What a nice ____________!	Was für ein schöner **Tag**!
8 The baby is four ____________ old.	Das Baby ist vier **Wochen** alt.
9 My first lesson ____________ is English.	Meine erste Stunde **am Montag** ist Englisch.

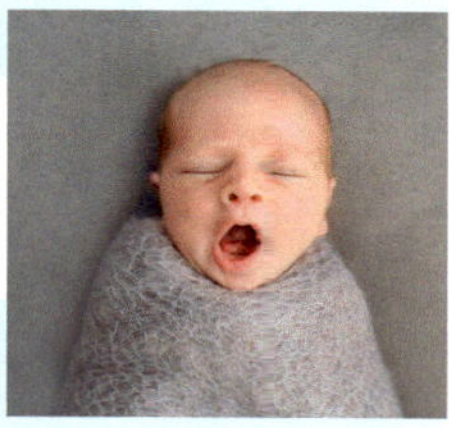

12 Opposites

Finde die Gegenteile.

1 (to) sit down ◄► ____________
2 Hello ◄► ____________
3 (to) open ◄► ____________
4 big ◄► ____________
5 right ◄► ____________
6 great ◄► ____________
7 old ◄► ____________
8 answer ◄► ____________

13 What's the right word: *is* or *are*?

Vervollständige die Sätze mit den sechs Wörtern aus dem Kasten.

Is • is • isn't • Are • are • 're

1 Sian and Ron ____________ friends.
2 ____________ this your book?
3 You ____________ nice, Scout!
4 Jack ____________ happy about the school uniform.
5 ____________ you from Brighton, Ron?
6 Where ____________ Sian from?

14 New words and phrases

▸ pp. 26–27 | VOCABULARY p. 244

1	Ruth has ten different ________________.	Ruth hat zehn verschiedene **Schulfächer**.
2	At __________________________ teachers ______________: Are all the students at school?	Bei der **Anwesenheitskontrolle überprüfen** die Lehrkräfte: Sind alle Schüler/innen in der Schule?
3	British school days often start with ________________.	Britische Schultage beginnen oft mit einer **Schulversammlung**.
4	Jake's favourite subject is ________________.	Jakes Lieblingsfach ist **Geschichte**.
5	Zoe and Philip like ________________.	Zoe und Philip mögen **Erdkunde**.
6	What's for ______________________?	Was gibt es zum **Mittagessen**?
7	Ms Evans is Zoe's ________________ teacher.	Frau Evans ist Zoes **Mathe**lehrerin.
8	________________ lessons are great.	**Naturwissenschafts**stunden sind toll.
9	________________________ is great too.	**Französisch** ist auch super.
10	I like ________________________________.	Ich mag **Werken**.
11	Rishi and Aaron love ________________.	Rishi und Aaron lieben **Informatik**.
12	________________ is my favourite subject.	**Sport** ist mein Lieblingsfach.
13	Zoe and Philip like ________________ lessons ________________ they like animals.	Zoe und Philip mögen **Biologie**stunden, **weil** sie Tiere mögen.
14	I think French is ________________.	Ich finde, dass Französisch **schwer** ist.
15	Ruby and Jamie like ________________ food. Ruby and Jamie's mum is ________________.	Ruby und Jamie mögen **deutsches** Essen. Rubys und Jamies Mama ist **Deutsche**.
16	My favourite place in school is the science __________________________.	Mein Lieblingsschulraum ist das **Labor**.

15 Scrambled words

Hier sind einige Buchstaben durcheinandergeraten. Schreibe die Wörter richtig auf.

1 Tom's favourite subject is *mpcotiung*. It's on *driaFy*. ________________________

2 *sHtoiry* is on *nydMoa*. ________________________

3 Lessons 3 and 4 on *Tuarhysd* are *aegghorpy*. ________________________

4 On *ndaSuy* we often play *otlbfoal*. ________________________

5 Sina's favourite subject is *cceeins*. It's on *ddseyneaW*. ________________________

6 On *rdauStay* Sina and Anna often go *lkiwang*. ________________________

7 Lessons 1 and 2 on *sedaTuy* are *enFhrc*. ________________________

16 New words and phrases

▸ pp. 28–29 | VOCABULARY p. 245

1	Brighton is a nice ________________.	Brighton ist ein netter **Ort**.
2	I walk to school ________________.	Ich laufe **allein** zur Schule.
3	________________ new house is big.	**Unser** neues Haus ist groß.
4	Put your books in your ________________.	Steck deine Bücher in deine **Tasche**.
5	Alfie has lunch in the ________________.	Alfie isst in der **Kantine** zu Mittag.
6	________________ we can have a pizza.	**Vielleicht** können wir eine Pizza essen.
7	Room 1A is in the first ________________.	Raum 1A ist im ersten **Korridor**.
8	"Look, there is a ________________."	„Schau, da ist eine **Landkarte**."
9	Rula's school is a big ________________.	Rulas Schule ist ein großes **Gebäude**.
10	The sports ________________ is cool.	Die Sport**halle** ist cool.
11	It's ________________ the canteen.	Sie ist **in der Nähe** der Kantine.
12	"I'm ________________ hungry now." –	„Ich bin jetzt **wirklich** hungrig." –
13	"You're ________________ hungry, Nick!"	„Du bist **immer** hungrig, Nick!"
14	The ________________ in our canteen is good.	Das **Essen** in unserer Kantine ist gut.
15	Suna is late. That's ________________.	Suna kommt zu spät. Das ist **schlecht**.
16	What day is ________________?	Welcher Tag ist **heute**?
17	My favourite ________________ is sport.	Meine Lieblings**aktivität** ist Sport.
18	Let's ________________ pizza for lunch.	Lass uns Pizza zum Mittagessen **besorgen**.

17 Our school

Beschrifte die Räume, Personen und Gegenstände.

1 ________________ 2 ________________ 3 ________________ 4 ________________

6 ________________ 7 ________________

5 ________________ 8 ________________ 9 ________________

18 New words and phrases

► p. 30 | VOCABULARY pp. 245–246

1	I often play football ______________ school.	Ich spiele oft Fußball **nach** der Schule.
2	Lola gets lots of books from the ______________.	Lola holt sich viele Bücher aus der **Bücherei**.
3	Can we play football in the ______________?	Können wir auf dem **Schulhof** Fußball spielen?
4	We often go to the ______________.	Wir gehen oft ins **Theater**.
5	Our sports hall is ______________ big.	Unsere Sporthalle ist **sehr** groß.
6	______________ and ______________ like reading.	**Oma** und **Opa** lesen gern.

19 New words and phrases

► p. 31 | VOCABULARY p. 246

1	In Britain, ______________ schools have a canteen.	In Großbritannien haben die **meisten** Schulen eine Mensa.
2	German students don't ______________ school uniforms.	Deutsche Schülerinnen und Schüler **tragen** keine Schuluniformen.
3	Do you want an apple ______________ a drink?	Möchtest du einen Apfel **oder** etwas zu trinken?
4	My new ______________ are grey and red.	Meine neue **Hose** ist grau und rot.
5	I don't like white ______________.	Ich mag keine weißen **Socken**.
6	I often wear ______________.	Ich trage oft **Röcke**.
7	Your ______________ are nice.	Deine **Schuhe** sind schön.
8	Tom ______________ a dog and two cats.	Tom **hat** einen Hund und zwei Katzen.
9	Grandma and Grandpa have a ______________.	Oma und Opa haben eine **Ziege**.
10	There are different ______________ at my school.	Es gibt verschiedene **Arbeitsgemeinschaften** an meiner Schule.
11	Please close the ______________.	Bitte mach das **Tor** zu.
12	I don't like you! Go ______________!	Ich mag dich nicht! Geh **weg**!
13	Can you ______________ me your phone number?	Kannst du mir deine Telefonnummer **geben**?
14	Grandma is always ______________.	Oma ist immer **freundlich**.
15	Ms Khan is a ______________ teacher.	Frau Khan ist eine **nette** Lehrerin.

20 New words and phrases

▸ p. 32 | VOCABULARY pp. 247–248

1	Ella isn't scared of big animals. She's a very ______________ girl.	Ella hat keine Angst vor großen Tieren. Sie ist ein sehr **mutiges** Mädchen.
2	Brady is a very ______________ student.	Brady ist ein sehr **hilfsbereiter** Schüler.
3	Don't be ______________ to your friends.	Sei nicht **gemein** zu deinen Freunden.
4	There are six different ______________ in the story.	Es gibt sechs **Figuren** in der Geschichte.
5	"______________ is that?" – "Our maths teacher."	„**Wer** ist das?" – „Unser Mathelehrer."
6	Jack is ______________ because he's alone.	Jack ist **traurig**, weil er allein ist.
7	Let's eat first, ______________ play football.	Lasst uns erst essen, **dann** Fußball spielen.
8	Take a sandwich. They're ______________.	Nimm dir ein Sandwich. Sie sind **kostenlos**.
9	British ______________ are great.	Britische **Strände** sind super.
10	Deva can't ______________.	Deva kann **sich** nicht **bewegen**.
11	Amy's bike is old and ______________.	Amys Fahrrad ist alt und **langsam**.
12	Don't put your scooter here. It's ______________ big.	Stell deinen Roller nicht hier hin. Er ist **zu** groß.
13	I don't understand this ______________ message.	Ich verstehe diese **seltsame** Nachricht nicht.
14	There's a horrible ______________ in class 5A.	In Klasse 5A gibt es einen schlimmen **Mobber**.
15	Brian, you're late again! You're in ______________ now.	Brian, du hast dich wieder verspätet! Du kriegst jetzt **Ärger**.
16	These are my books, ______________ are your books.	Dies sind meine Bücher, **die dort** sind deine Bücher.
17	I don't like horses. I'm scared of ______________.	Ich mag Pferde nicht. Ich habe Angst vor **ihnen**.
18	Tolga and ______________ of his friends often play football after school.	Tolga und **einige** seiner Freunde spielen oft Fußball nach der Schule.

21 New words and phrases

▸ pp. 33–34 | VOCABULARY p. 248

1	Harry is nice. I often play with __________.	Harry ist nett. Ich spiele oft mit **ihm**.
2	"Where are you?" – "__________ at school."	„Wo bist du?" – „**Noch** in der Schule."
3	Rula and __________ friend like dancing.	Rula und **ihre** Freundin tanzen gern.
4	Sam and __________ dad are on holiday.	Sam und **sein** Papa sind im Urlaub.
5	__________.	**Das hier sind meine Freunde/Freundinnen.**
6	__________ you are my friend, George!	**Ich bin froh, dass** du mein Freund bist, George!
7	My __________ lesson on Monday is English.	Meine **erste** Stunde am Montag ist Englisch.
8	Luis and his friends like __________.	Luis und seine Freunde **schauspielern** gern.
9	Your music is too __________!	Eure Musik ist zu **laut**!
10	Our school is too big. What's your __________?	Unsere Schule ist zu groß. Was ist deine **Meinung**?
11	Our __________ lesson is art.	In der **nächsten** Stunde haben wir Kunst.

22 New words and phrases

▸ p. 36 | VOCABULARY pp. 248–249

1	You can use your phone to __________ new __________.	Du kannst dein Handy benutzen, um neuen **Wortschatz** zu **lernen**.
2	Making a __________ can be helpful too.	Ein **Wörternetz** anzulegen kann auch hilfreich sein.
3	What's a good __________ to learn to play the guitar?	Was ist eine gute **Art und Weise**, Gitarre spielen zu lernen?
4	Make a __________ for all your school subjects on your computer.	Lege einen **Ordner** für alle Schulfächer auf deinem Computer an.
5	The English __________ for "Elefant" is "elephant".	Das englische **Wort** für „Elefant" ist „elephant".
6	British students __________ 11 __________ 16 go to secondary school.	Britische Schülerinnen und Schüler **von** 11 **bis** 16 gehen auf eine weiterführende Schule.

23 New words and phrases

► p. 37 | VOCABULARY p. 249

1	Let's ______________ a poster.	Lasst uns ein Poster **machen**.
2	Careful, there's a ______________.	Vorsicht, da ist eine **Stufe**.
3	A hat can be very ______________.	Ein Hut kann sehr **nützlich** sein.
4	Always ask people ______________ ______________.	Frag die Leute immer, **bevor du ein Foto machst!**
5	Coding is ______________.	Programmieren ist **schwierig**.

24 Listen carefully!

03

Höre dir die Sätze aufmerksam an und schreibe das fehlende Wort in die Lücke.

1 Rishi is Jay's best ______________.

2 ______________ in the same class.

3 They like ______________ school subjects.

4 Jay's ______________ subject is history,

5 Rishi's is ______________.

6 Jay and Rishi think maths is ______________.

7 In Rishi's ______________ German isn't hard.

8 Jay and Rishi like the ______________.

9 They eat lunch in the ______________.

10 But the food ______________ always nice.

25 Let's talk: Über Freunde/Freundinnen und den Schulalltag sprechen

► pp. 225 and 228

Hilf Melissa ihre beste Freundin zu beschreiben. Verwende die Ausdrücke aus dem Kasten.

alone • because • best friend • happy • helpful • lucky • nice • same class • students • too • very • years old

This is Mia. She's ten ______________ ______________.

I'm ten ______________. We're in the ______________ ______________.

Mia is my ______________ ______________ She's always

______________. The other ______________ in my class are

______________ too. I'm ______________ ______________ I'm not

______________. I'm a ______________ ______________ girl

Unit 2
My family and home

1 New words and phrases

▸ pp. 50–51 | VOCABULARY pp. 249–250

1	Luca's ____________ is from London.	Lucas **Familie** kommt aus London.
2	Harper's ____________ is in Brighton.	Harper's **Zuhause** ist in Brighton.
3	Luca's ____________ Anne is from London too.	Lucas **Tante** Anne kommt auch aus London.
4	Luca's ____________ Tao is from China.	Lucas **Onkel** Tao kommt aus China.
5	Lisa has two ____________: Rob and Joe.	Lisa hat zwei **Brüder**: Rob und Joe.
6	Tom has a ____________. Her name is Cara.	Tom hat eine **Schwester**. Sie heißt Cara.
7	Lisa's ____________ Mandy is from Jena.	Lisas **Cousine** Mandy ist aus Jena.
8	Sam's ____________ Martin is from Berlin.	Sams **Cousin** Martin ist aus Berlin.
9	The Browns have a ____________ and a ____________.	Die Browns haben eine **Tochter** und einen **Sohn**.
10	Please draw a ____________.	Bitte zeichne einen **Kreis**.
11	Sam's ____________ have a big dog.	Sams **Nachbarn** haben einen großen Hund.
12	Sarah's ____________ is nice.	Sarahs **Stiefmutter** ist nett.
13	Sam loves Lisa. They can ____________.	Sam liebt Lisa. Sie können **heiraten**.
14	Chris is ____________ Paul.	Chris ist **mit** Paul **verheiratet**.

2 Lost words

Vervollständige die Sätze mit den Wörtern aus den Luftballons.

1 You can answer the question _in_ different ways.
2 Lisa and Sam aren't ____________ school.
3 Julia's family is ____________ Germany.
4 What's the English word ____________ "Aufgabe"?
5 I go swimming ____________ Mondays.
6 I like the colour ____________ your bike.
7 You can sit ____________ here.

3 Family words

Trage das Wort, das in den Sätzen fehlt, in das Gitter ein.

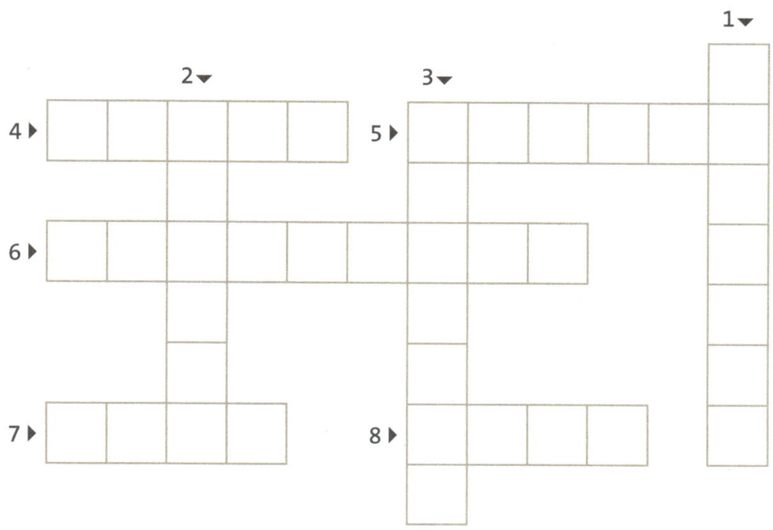

1 Molly's ??? is two years old. His name is John.
2 Molly's ??? Moira is 10. Her mum is Molly's mum's sister Hannah.
3 Molly's mum's new partner is Harry. He is Molly's ???.
4 Molly's dad's brother is Molly's ???.
5 Molly's dad has a ??? too. Her name is Carol.
6 Molly's grandma Janet has two ???: Hannah and Molly's mum Laura.
7 Molly's other grandma Susan has two ??? and one daughter.
8 Carol is Molly and John's ???.

4 New words and phrases

▸ pp. 52–53 | VOCABULARY pp. 250–251

1	A cat is a good ____________.	Eine Katze ist ein gutes **Haustier**.
2	Lucy and Sam have ____________ friends.	Lucy und Sam haben **viele** Freunde.
3	Kim's ____________ is always hungry.	Kims **Kaninchen** ist immer hungrig.
4	____________ like being alone.	**Hamster** sind gern allein.
5	________________________?	**Hast du dich verlaufen/verirrt?**
6	Mike is ____________ because he can't have a pet.	Mike ist **wütend**, weil er kein Haustier haben kann.
7	A ____________ helps animals.	Ein **Tierarzt** / Eine **Tierärztin** hilft Tieren.
8	There is no school at the ____________, ____________ I can play with my dogs.	Am **Wochenende** ist keine Schule. **Also** kann ich mit meinen Hunden spielen.
9	Ms Fox likes her ____________. She's a maths teacher.	Frau Fox mag ihre **Arbeit** gern. Sie ist Mathelehrerin.
10	Ruth's ____________ is big and old.	Ruths **Haus** ist groß und alt.
11	Tom is very ____________.	Tom ist sehr **unordentlich**.
12	Joe is a helpful and ____________ boy.	Joe ist ein hilfsbereiter und **höflicher** Junge.
13	Carl and Eric have ____________ one laptop.	Carl und Eric haben **nur** einen Laptop.

5 New words and phrases

▶ p. 54 | VOCABULARY p. 251

1	Today Carl can't play football because he has a lot of ______________.	Carl kann heute nicht Fußball spielen, weil er viele **Hausaufgaben** hat.
2	Jake is sad. His dog is ______________.	Jake ist traurig. Sein Hund wird **vermisst**.
3	Horses can't ______________.	Pferde können nicht **fliegen**.
4	Please ______________ me ______________ you're home.	Bitte **ruf** mich **an**, **wenn** du zu Hause bist.
5	______________ you like the book, you can have it.	**Wenn** du das Buch magst, kannst du es haben.
6	Mandy can't ______________ her phone.	Mandy kann ihr Handy nicht **finden**.

6 Bits and pieces

Verbinde die Teile miteinander, um Wörter zu bilden.

1 daugh | 2 step | 3 neigh | 4 week | 5 home | 6 po | 7 rab | 8 ham

bour | work | bit | lite | ter | end | ster | mum

7 New words and phrases

▶ p. 55 | VOCABULARY pp. 251–252

1	Ria and her brother ______________ new bikes.	Ria und ihr Bruder **wollen** neue Fahrräder.
2	Ria and her brother are very ______________. They do lots of sports.	Ria und ihr Bruder sind sehr **aktiv**. Sie treiben viel Sport.
3	Tom's baby brother is really ______________.	Toms kleiner Bruder ist wirklich **niedlich**.
4	Horses can be very ______________.	Pferde können sehr **schnell** sein.
5	I think maths is ______________.	Ich finde, dass Mathe **interessant** ist.
6	Ji-Ho's sandwiches are really ______________.	Ji-Ho's Sandwiches sind etwas **Besonderes**.
7	A ______________ is a reptile.	Eine **Eidechse** ist ein Reptil.
8	Coding is ______________ hard.	Programmieren ist **ziemlich** schwer.
9	What's your ______________ pet?	Welches ist dein **Traum**haustier?

8 New words and phrases

▶ p. 56 | VOCABULARY p. 252

1 I like the apple __________ in Grandma's __________.	Ich mag die Apfel**bäume** in Omas **Garten**.
2 Our building is very big. We're on the __________.	Unser Haus ist sehr groß. Wir wohnen im **Erdgeschoss**.
3 Uncle Peter is on the __________.	Onkel Peter wohnt im **Dachgeschoss**.
4 Uncle Peter's __________ is small, but it has a __________.	Onkel Peters **Wohnung** ist klein, aber sie hat einen **Balkon**.
5 There are two __________.	Es gibt zwei **Garagen**.
6 __________ room in our flat is different.	**Jedes** Zimmer in unserer Wohnung ist anders.
7 I like the old __________ in my room.	Ich mag die alte **Lampe** in meinem Zimmer.
8 Lara has __________ brothers or sisters.	Lara hat **keine** Geschwister.

9 New words and phrases

▶ p. 57 | VOCABULARY pp. 252–253

1 Here's a __________ of Ella's house: — Hier ist ein **Rundgang** durch Ellas Haus:

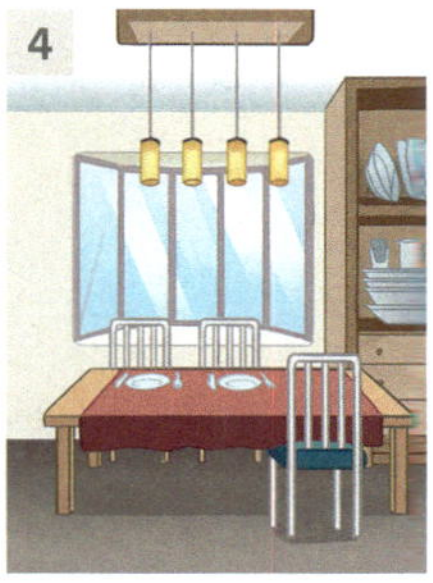

2 __________

3 __________

4 __________

5 __________

6 __________

7 __________

10 The fourth word

Ergänze das fehlende Wort.

1 aunt – uncle → sister – __________

2 dad – mum → son – __________

3 slow – fast → quiet – __________

4 good – bad → kind – __________

5 parrot – fly → fish – __________

11 Listen carefully!

04

Höre dir die Sätze aufmerksam an und schreibe das fehlende Wort in die Lücke.

1 Please draw a ______________________.
2 Our cat is very ______________________.
3 My sister is ______________________ loud.
4 My brother is a very ______________________ boy.
5 Our ______________________ are very nice.
6 A lizard is a very ______________________ pet.
7 Fish are ______________________ pets.
8 What's your ______________________ pet?

12 New words and phrases

► p. 58 | VOCABULARY p. 253

1 When it's ____________, I go swimming.	Wenn es **sonnig** ist, gehe ich schwimmen.
2 We have a very ____________ flat.	Wir haben eine sehr **moderne** Wohnung.
3 Liam and Aira ____________ in the same ____________.	Liam und Aira **wohnen** in derselben **Straße**.
4 __________ the class what books you read.	**Erzähle** der Klasse, welche Bücher du liest.

13 New words and phrases

► p. 59 | VOCABULARY p. 253

1 We live in a new ______________________.	Wir wohnen in einem neuen **Mehrfamilienhaus**.
2 Harry's family has a ______________________ ____________.	Harrys Familie hat ein **Reihenhaus**.
3 Rishi's family has a big ____________ ______________________.	Rishis Familie hat ein großes **freistehendes Haus**.
4 I would like to live in a ____________ ______________________.	Ich würde gern in einer **Doppelhaushälfte** wohnen.
5 Tom and Sam like ____________ English teacher.	Tom und Sam mögen **ihren** Englischlehrer.
6 Can you ____________ your bike to me?	Kannst du mir dein Fahrrad **beschreiben**?
7 We have a ______________________ near Brighton.	Wir haben ein **Häuschen** in der Nähe von Brighton.
8 Who is the ____________ boy there?	Wer ist der **kleine** Junge dort?

14 New words and phrases

▸ p. 60 | VOCABULARY pp. 253–254

Sieh dir die Bilder an, lies die Sätze und trage die richtigen Wörter in das Gitter ein.

1

The dog is ??? the house.

2

3

The cat is ??? the bed.

4

There are two ??? in Jim's bedroom.

6

5

The little boy is ??? his mum and dad.

7

8

9

10

11

The little boy is ??? the tree.

12

13

There's a lamp ??? the table.

14

15

16

There's a garage ??? our house.

17

There are pens on the ???.

15 New words and phrases

▸ pp. 61–63 | VOCABULARY p. 254

1 Please close the ________________.	Bitte schließe die **Tür**.
2 Julia is quite messy, but her sister is very ________________.	Julia ist ziemlich unordentlich, aber ihre Schwester ist sehr **ordentlich**.
3 Ms Berry is a very nice ________________.	Frau Berry ist eine sehr nette **Person**.
4 Lara and Sina love ________________.	Lara und Sina lieben **Süßigkeiten**.
5 Ron's pet is always in ________________ ________________.	Rons Haustier ist immer in **seinem Terrarium**.
6 Our house is big, so I have ________________ ________________ room.	Unser Haus ist groß, sodass ich **ein eigenes** Zimmer habe.
7 What colour are the ________________ in your room?	Welche Farbe haben die **Wände** in deinem Zimmer?

16 New words and phrases

▸ p. 64 | VOCABULARY p. 255

1 Houses in London are very ________________.	Häuser in London sind sehr **teuer**.
2 "Can we meet on Monday?" – "Yes, Monday is ________________."	„Können wir uns am Montag treffen?" – „Ja, Montag ist **perfekt**."
3 I can help you at weekends. Is that ________________?	Ich kann dir an Wochenenden helfen. Ist das **genug**?
4 When Harry has a ________________ with maths, he can ask his sister.	Wenn Harry ein **Problem** mit Mathe hat, kann er seine Schwester fragen.
5 Sarah's ________________ are teachers.	Sarahs **Eltern** sind Lehrer.
6 "Can I use your bathroom?" – "________________!"	„Darf ich Ihr Bad benutzen?" – „**Natürlich**!"
7 Alfie's dad is really ________________.	Alfies Papa ist wirklich **witzig**.
8 I ________________ English and German.	Ich **spreche** Englisch und Deutsch.
9 Bye, Leroy. ________________.	Tschüs, Leroy. **Bis später.**

17 Odd word out

Unterstreiche das Wort, das nicht in die Reihe passt.

1 angry – loud – polite – vet – cute – fast

2 rabbit – dream – hamster – lizard – snake

3 chocolate – sweets – tree – apple – sandwich

4 chair – cushion – bed – shelf – wardrobe

18 Lost words

Vervollständige die Sätze mit dem richtigen Wort. Verwende die Wörter aus dem Kasten.

he • her • his • I • it • its • my • our • she • their • they • you (2x) • your (2x)

– Are 1 ___________ new here? Is this 2 ___________ house? I think 3 ___________ is very nice.

– I'm Amy. This is 4 ___________ house. This is 5 ___________ sister. 6 ___________ is five years old.

7 ___________ name is Joanna. And this is my brother Joel. 8 ___________ is twelve.

9 ___________ hobby is swimming. My parents are teachers. 10 ___________ are always busy.

11 ___________ names are Kate and Ron. And this is our garden. 12 ___________ love it.

13 ___________ trees have a lot of apples.

– It's nice that 14 ___________ are our neighbours now. Maybe we can play in 15 ___________ garden.

19 New words and phrases

► p. 65 | VOCABULARY p. 255

1	___________________ is ready!	Das **Abendessen** ist fertig!
2	What's wrong, ___________________?	Was ist los, **Liebling**?
3	Don't be ___________________!	Sei nicht **unhöflich**!
4	Our dog is ___________________ of our family.	Unser Hund ist **Teil** unserer Familie.
5	Lots of people have ___________________ bikes.	Viele Leute haben **Elektro**fahrräder.
6	Your music is very loud. Please use your ___________________.	Deine Musik ist sehr laut. Bitte benutze deinen **Kopfhörer**.
7	We often play ___________________ on Sunday.	Wir spielen oft **Spiele** am Sonntag.
8	We're ___________________ from our holiday.	Wir sind **zurück** aus dem Urlaub.

20 What's the right word: *have* or *has*?

Vervollständige die Sätze mit dem richtigen Wort.

1 Maja ___________ a dog.
2 Sarah ___________ two sisters.
3 Mr and Mrs Owen ___________ a big garden.
4 Sina always ___________ lots of homework.
5 I ___________ a brother.
6 We ___________ no pets.

21 New words and phrases

► p. 66 | VOCABULARY pp. 255–256

1 "Who is _____________ ?" – "Dad."	„Wer ist **am Telefon**?" – „Papa."
2 "Can we go for a walk?" – "Yes, that's a good _____________ !"	„Können wir spazieren gehen?" – „Ja, das ist eine gute **Idee**."
3 What's that horrible _____________ ?	Was ist das für ein fürchterlicher **Lärm**?
4 When I call my cousin in London, we always talk for a _____________ time.	Wenn ich meinen Cousin in London anrufe, sprechen wir immer **lange** miteinander.
5 Let's find a _____________ to this problem.	Lasst uns eine **Lösung** für dieses Problem finden.

22 Opposites

Finde die Gegenteile.

1 tidy ◄► _____________

2 active ◄► _____________

3 slow ◄► _____________

4 on ◄► _____________

5 polite ◄► _____________

23 New words and phrases

► p. 68 | VOCABULARY p. 256

1 Can you _____________ your name?	Kannst du deinen Namen **buchstabieren**?
2 Learn the _____________ .	Lerne das **Alphabet**.
3 What's your _____________ ?	Wie lautet deine **Adresse**?
4 "Can I feed your lizard?" – "Yes, do it _____________ ."	„Kann ich deine Eidechse füttern?" – „Ja, mach es **so**."
5 My phone number is _________ one five ...	Meine Telefonnummer ist **null** eins fünf ...
6 _________ your favourite word from this unit.	**Schreib** dein Lieblingswort aus dieser Unit.

24 New words and phrases

► p. 69 | VOCABULARY p. 256

1 _____________ your dream pet.	**Präsentiere** dein Traumhaustier.
2 My brother is a _____________ .	Mein Bruder ist **Fotograf**.

25 Lost words

Vervollständige die Sätze mit den Wörtern aus den Luftballons.

1 Paul and Liv want ___to___ have a hamster.

2 Grandma and Grandpa have a lot ________ apple trees in their garden.

3 Tess lives ________ her dad and her stepmum.

4 Rishi and his dad often play tennis ________ the weekend.

5 What's special ________ lizards?

6 Joel and his sister live ________ the top floor.

7 We go to school ________ Monday ________ Friday.

8 Say it ________ English, please.

26 Listen carefully!

05

Höre dir die Sätze aufmerksam an und schreibe das fehlende Wort in die Lücke.

1 My brother is ________________ years old.

2 My dad is ________________.

3 Grandma is ________________.

4 Louis is ________________.

5 Our house is ________________.

6 ________________ are four big bedrooms.

7 My brothers love ________________ bedroom.

8 Mum and Dad love our ________________.

9 Our bikes are in one of the two ________________.

10 I love the trees in our big ________________.

27 That's wrong!

Die Aussagen sind falsch. Verbessere die Fehler. Schreibe ganze Sätze.

1 Your uncle is your mother's sister. ________________.

2 People cook their food in the bathroom. ________________.

3 Rabbits can fly. ________________.

4 Lions are good pets. ________________.

28 Let's talk: Das eigene Zuhause beschreiben

▸ pp. 226–227

Sieh dir das Bild an und beschrifte es. Verwende die Wörter aus dem Kasten.

balcony • bathroom • bedroom • dining room • garden • ground floor / first floor • kitchen • living room • garage

1 ____________

2 ____________

3 ____________

4 ____________

5 ____________

6 ____________

7 ____________

8 ____________

9 ____________

10 ____________

Beschreibe das Haus nun einer anderen Person. Du kannst deine Beschreibung auch aufnehmen und jemanden bitten, sich deine Tonaufnahme anzuhören und dir Feedback zu geben.

I can see a ____________ in the picture. There are ____________ floors. On the ground ____________, there is a ____________, a ____________ and a ____________. On the ____________, there are ____________ ____________. There is a ____________ next to the parents' bedroom. In the garage, I see ____________. There is a ____________ with ____________.

Unit 3
My day

1 New words and phrases

▸ pp. 84–85 | VOCABULARY pp. 256–257

1 How long is your school ____________?	Wie lang ist dein Schul**weg**?
2 Can you ____________ to my party?	Kannst du zu meiner Party **kommen**?
3 Liam and Tom take the same ____________ to school.	Liam und Tom fahren mit demselben **Bus** zur Schule.
4 Lots of students go to school ____________ ____________.	Viele Schüler und Schülerinnen fahren **mit dem Fahrrad** zur Schule.
5 Lots of teachers come ____________.	Viele Lehrer kommen **mit dem Auto**.
6 We go to the beach ____________.	Wir fahren **mit dem Zug** zum Strand.
7 Can I take a ____________ break?	Kann ich eine **kurze** Pause machen?

2 New words and phrases

▸ p. 86 | VOCABULARY p. 257

1 We only open on ____________.	Wir öffnen nur an **Werktagen**.
2 Can we meet ____________?	Können wir uns **um 10 Uhr** treffen?
3 Joe's swimming class is ____________.	Joes Schwimmkurs ist **um 5 Uhr nachmittags**.
4 Our house is very quiet ____________.	Unser Haus ist sehr still **um 2 Uhr morgens**.
5 Brighton is in the ____________.	Brighton ist im **Vereinigten Königreich**.
6 I only work five ____________ on Mondays.	Ich arbeite montags nur fünf **Stunden**.
7 Mandy's grandparents have a big old ____________ in their living room.	Mandys Großeltern haben eine große alte **Uhr** im Wohnzimmer.
8 I walk to work ____________ and take the bus home ____________.	Ich laufe **morgens** zur Arbeit und fahre **abends** mit dem Bus nach Hause.
9 Tom has guitar lessons on Monday ____________.	Tom hat am Montag**nachmittag** Gitarrenunterricht.
10 I meet Joe ____________.	Ich treffe mich mit Joe **zur Mittagszeit**.
11 I don't like the ____________ of the story.	Ich mag das **Ende** der Geschichte nicht.
12 ____________	**Wie spät ist es?**

3 New words and phrases

▸ p. 87 | VOCABULARY pp. 257–258

1	________________ are you late again?	**Warum** hast du dich wieder verspätet?
2	My parents always read the ____________ in the morning.	Meine Eltern lesen morgens immer **Zeitung**.
3	My grandma still writes ____________.	Meine Oma schreibt noch **Briefe**.
4	Mike is in a swimming ____________.	Mike nimmt an einem Schimm**wettbewerb** teil.
5	Dilek is Lara's ____________ friend.	Dilek ist Laras **beste** Freundin.
6	"Bike or bus?" – "You can ____________."	„Fahrrad oder Bus?" – „Du kannst **wählen**."
7	Lara is the ____________ of the maths competition. She often ____________ competitions.	Lara ist die **Gewinnerin** des Mathematik-wettbewerbs. Sie **gewinnt** oft Wettbewerbe.
8	Moira has a bad ____________.	Moira hat eine schwere **Krankheit**.
9	Yuri has a ____________.	Yuri hat einen **Rollstuhl**.
10	Laura's ____________ is a teacher.	Lauras **Ehemann** ist Lehrer.
11	Shaun and Sophie work in a ____________.	Shaun und Sophie arbeiten in einem **Café**.
12	On weekdays, I ____________ at 7 a.m.	An Wochentagen **stehe** ich um 7 Uhr **auf**.
13	A lot of students ____________ after PE.	Viele Schülerinnen und Schüler **duschen** nach dem Sportunterricht.
14	Tom, it's time to ____________!	Tom, es ist Zeit, **sich anzuziehen**!
15	____________ is from 7 a.m. to 10 a.m.	**Frühstück** ist von 7 bis 10 Uhr.
16	The films ____________ an hour.	Die Filme **dauern** eine Stunde.
17	Can we ____________ the swimming competition?	Können wir uns den Schwimmwettbewerb **anschauen**?

4 Bits and pieces

Verbinde die Teile miteinander, um Wörter zu bilden.

1 week   2 morn   3 jour   4 lunch   5 even   6 wheel   7 hus   8 news

ney   time   paper   chair   ing   band   day   ing

5 Lost words

Vervollständige die Sätze mit den Wörtern aus dem Kasten.

How • What • When • Where • Who • Why

1 ______________________ is breakfast?
2 ______________________ are you sad?
3 ______________________ is your favourite animal?
4 ______________________ old is your brother?
5 ______________________ is the canteen?
6 ______________________ is your English teacher?

6 New words and phrases

▸ pp. 88–89 | VOCABULARY pp. 258–259

1 Look at the words in ______________________ 5.	Schau dir die Wörter in **Zeile** 5 an.
2 Can we ______________________ now?	Können wir jetzt **einkaufen gehen**?
3 Louis and his dad ______________________ their ______________________.	Louis und sein Vater **putzen sich** die **Zähne**.
4 My baby brother only has one ______________________.	Mein kleiner Bruder hat erst einen **Zahn**.
5 ______________________ can be in the maths competition.	**Jeder** kann am Mathematikwettbewerb teilnehmen.
6 Please choose a ______________________.	Bitte wählt ein **Projekt** aus.
7 Mr Brown lives in the ______________________.	Mr Brown wohnt auf dem **Land**.

7 Listen carefully!

06

Höre dir die Sätze aufmerksam an und schreibe das fehlende Wort in die Lücke.

1 It's a long ______________________ from Tom's home to his grandparents' house.
2 It takes eight ______________________.
3 They live in the ______________________.
4 Tom's dad lives in Germany, his mum in the ______________________.
5 Tom and his sister are in an art ______________________.

8 New words and phrases

► p. 90 | VOCABULARY p. 259

1	At Lara's school, students can choose from different clubs. A lot of them choose ____________.	An Laras Schule können die Schüler/innen aus verschiedenen AGs auswählen. Viele von ihnen wählen **Schauspiel**.
2	Sina often ____________ to school.	Sina **fährt** oft mit dem **Rad** zur Schule.
3	My family loves ____________.	Meine Familie liebt das **Wandern**.
4	Phil's favourite sport is ____________.	Phils Lieblingssport ist **Laufen**.
5	Anna thinks ____________ is great.	Anna findet **Trampolinspringen** toll.
6	____________ club is your favourite?	**Welche** AG ist dein Favorit?
7	Lara wants to ____________ the tennis club.	Lara möchte in einen Tennisverein **eintreten**.
8	Let me show you ____________ hold the baby.	Lass mich dir zeigen, **wie man** das Baby hält.
9	I go and see my grandma ____________ Sunday.	Ich besuche meine Oma **jeden** Sonntag.
10	What's your favourite ____________?	Was ist dein Lieblings**monat**?
11	Stella's grandpa lives ____________.	Stellas Opa lebt **am Meer**.
12	Mia has an ____________ job. She's a pilot.	Mia hat einen **aufregenden** Beruf. Sie ist Pilotin.

9 Lost words

Vervollständige die Sätze mit den Wörtern aus den Luftballons.

1 *On* weekdays, Luana gets 2 ____________ 3 ____________ 7 a.m. She has a shower 4 ____________ she gets dressed. Then she has breakfast 5 ____________ the kitchen with her family. She walks 6 ____________ school with her brother. School starts 7 ____________ 9 a.m. There are three lessons 8 ____________ the morning, and three 9 ____________ lunch. 10 ____________ lunchtime, Luana meets her friends 11 ____________ the canteen. 12 ____________ the end of the school day, Luana goes home 13 ____________ bus. 14 ____________ the bus she often listens 15 ____________ music.

ADVANCED lighthouse 1

Wordmaster

Lösungen

Cornelsen

Hello!

1 New words and phrases
▸ pp. 10–11 | VOCABULARY pp. 234–235

1 Hello. • **2** Nice to meet you. • **3** nice • **4** Meet • **5** you • **6** I'm / I am • **7** I'm / I am hungry. • **8** Careful • **9** a seagull • **10** It's / It is • **11** The • **12** What's your name? • **13** Hi. / Hello. • **14** number • **15** year old • **16** How old are you? • **17** Where are you from? • **18** like • **19** What about you? • **20** football • **21** thank you / thanks • **22** colour • **23** and • **24** right; wrong • **25** class • **26** too • **27** Bye. • **28** Goodbye.

2 Colours
▸ p. 12 | VOCABULARY p. 235

1 red • **2** blue • **3** white • **4** brown • **5** grey • **6** yellow • **7** green • **8** purple • **9** black • **10** orange • **11** pink

3 Let's talk: Sich und andere vorstellen
▸ p. 225 and p. 227

Hi / Hello! I'm ***[dein Name]***. I'm 10. **How old** are you? • Nice to **meet you too**. I'm from ***[dein Wohnort]***. Where **are you from**? • **Bye. / Goodbye.**

4 New words and phrases
▸ pp. 12–13 | VOCABULARY pp. 235–236

1 on holiday • **2** Mum; Dad; picture • **3** Tom's mum • **4** animals • **5** drinks; things to eat • **6** other things • **7** Here; can see • **8** can't/cannot see • **9** Remember; dogs • **10** How are you? • **11** I'm fine. • **12** I'm not • **13** so good

5 Plurals

1 two dogs • **2** four footballs • **3** three seagulls • **4** five drinks

6 New words and phrases
▸ p. 14 | VOCABULARY p. 236

1 about me/you/Tom • **2** My favourite • **3** There are; my • **4** cat • **5** an elephant • **6** horse • **7** lions, monkeys, parrots; snakes • **8** fish

7 Picture crossword: animals

1 cat • **2** seagull • **3** snake • **4** lion • **5** dog • **6** fish • **7** horse • **8** elephant • **9** parrot • **10** monkey

8 New words and phrases
▸ p. 15 | VOCABULARY pp. 236–237

1 hobby • **2** sport • **3** Listen to • **4** music • **5** draw • **6** dancing • **7** swim • **8** photo • **9** take photos • **10** love • **11** don't like • **12** guitar • **13** bike • **14** cap • **15** chain • **16** book • **17** phone • **18** scooter • **19** small • **20** new • **21** big • **22** This; gold • **23** silver • **24** with • **25** read • **26** Put

9 Listen carefully!

1 elephant • **2** horse • **3** monkey • **4** parrot • **5** snake • **6** guitar • **7** yellow • **8** favourite

10 New words and phrases
▸ p. 16 | VOCABULARY p. 238

1 but • **2** of my • **3** all • **4** do • **5** hat • **6** singing • **7** sorry • **8** That's

11 New words and phrases

► p. 17 | VOCABULARY pp. 238–239

1 ready • **2** for • **3** school • **4** please; quiet • **5** stand up • **6** sit down • **7** look at; board • **8** open • **9** put your hand up / put up your hand • **10** Close

12 Listen carefully!

1 phone • **2** ready • **3** Where • **4** Listen • **5** bike • **6** photo • **7** Careful • **8** What's

13 Word search

1 meet • **2** How • **3** ten • **4** class • **5** pink

14 New at Park School

1 eleven; dancing; reading • **2** twelve; bike and scooter • **3** thirteen; football and (listening to) music

15 Numbers

1 four • **2** three • **3** fourteen • **4** eight • **5** seven • **6** five • **7** two • **8** ten • **9** one

16 Let's talk: Über Hobbys, Vorlieben und Abneigungen sprechen

► p. 226

Hi! I'm ***[dein Name]***. I'm in class ***[deine Klasse]***. What's your **favourite** sport? • **I like / My favourite sport is *[dein Lieblingssport]*.** • **I like / My hobby is *[was du magst]*.** • **My favourite animal is *[dein Lieblingstier]*. I don't like *[Tiere, die du nicht magst]*.**

Unit 1: My new school

1 New words and phrases

► pp. 18–19 | VOCABULARY p. 239

1 coding • **2** walk • **3** cooking • **4** students • **5** at

2 New words and phrases

► p. 20 | VOCABULARY pp. 239–240

1 Time • **2** girl • **3** boy • **4** friend • **5** are friends • **6** busy • **7** tired • **8** tie • **9** is scared of • **10** (school) uniform • **11** the same • **12** know • **13** British • **14** have • **15** often • **16** great • **17** horrible

3 New words and phrases

► p. 21 | VOCABULARY p. 240

1 folder • **2** apple • **3** pencil case • **4** desk • **5** pen • **6** rubber • **7** exercise book • **8** English • **9** ruler • **10** glue stick • **11** art • **12** pencil sharpener

4 Odd word out

1 photo • **2** drink • **3** great • **4** apple • **5** horrible • **6** guitar

5 New words and phrases

► p. 22 | VOCABULARY pp. 240–241

1 different • **2** Mr; Mrs/Ms • **3** teachers • **4** I'm late • **5** don't be late • **6** again • **7** window • **8** Yes • **9** no • **10** go • **11** to • **12** toilet • **13** now • **14** take • **15** say • **16** talk • **17** Let's / Let us • **18** us • **19** Start • **20** secondary school

6 New words and phrases

► p. 23 | VOCABULARY pp. 241–242

1 in class • **2** What page • **3** page/p. • **4** understand • **5** help • **6** question • **7** answer to your question • **8** use • **9** here you are • **10** You're welcome. • **11** Ask • **12** classroom

7 Lost words

1 go • **2** draw • **3** play • **4** start • **5** use • **6** open

8 Word snake

1 same • **2** friend • **3** coding • **4** often • **5** teacher • **6** pencil

9 New words and phrases

► p. 24 | VOCABULARY pp. 242–243

1 timetable • **2** lesson • **3** They're / They are • **4** They aren't / They are not • **5** room • **6** is asleep • **7** He's / He is • **8** He isn't / He is not • **9** I think • **10** You're right / You are right • **11** She's / She is • **12** We're / We are • **13** breaks • **14** soon • **15** minutes • **16** people

10 Letter code

1 t • **2** h • **3** o • **4** r

11 New words and phrases

► p. 25 | VOCABULARY pp. 243–244

1 message • **2** are lucky • **3** See you. • **4** Dear • **5** is fun • **6** Yours • **7** day • **8** weeks • **9** on Monday

12 Opposites

1 (to) stand up • **2** Goodbye/Bye • **3** (to) close • **4** small • **5** wrong • **6** horrible • **7** new • **8** question

13 What's the word: *is* or *are*?

1 are • **2** Is • **3** 're • **4** isn't • **5** Are • **6** is

14 New words and phrases

► pp. 26–27 | VOCABULARY p. 244

1 (school) subjects • **2** registration; check • **3** assembly • **4** history • **5** geography • **6** lunch • **7** maths • **8** Science • **9** French • **10** design and technology • **11** computing • **12** PE / Physical education • **13** biology; because • **14** hard • **15** German; German • **16** laboratory

15 Scrambled words

1 computing; Friday • **2** History; Monday • **3** Thursday; geography • **4** Sunday; football • **5** science; Wednesday • **6** Saturday; walking • **7** Tuesday; French

16 New words and phrases
▸ pp. 28–29 | VOCABULARY p. 245

1 place • 2 alone • 3 Our • 4 bag • 5 canteen • 6 Maybe • 7 corridor • 8 map • 9 building • 10 hall • 11 near • 12 really • 13 always • 14 food • 15 bad • 16 today • 17 activity • 18 get

17 Our school

1 classroom • 2 books • 3 teacher • 4 sports hall • 5 canteen • 6 students • 7 window • 8 desk • 9 corridor

18 New words and phrases
▸ p. 30 | VOCABULARY pp. 245–246

1 after • 2 library • 3 playground • 4 theatre • 5 very • 6 Grandma; Grandpa

19 New words and phrases
▸ p. 31 | VOCABULARY p. 246

1 most • 2 wear • 3 or • 4 trousers • 5 socks • 6 skirts • 7 shoes • 8 has • 9 goat • 10 (school) clubs • 11 gate • 12 away • 13 give • 14 friendly • 15 kind

20 New words and phrases
▸ p. 32 | VOCABULARY pp. 247–248

1 brave • 2 helpful • 3 mean • 4 characters • 5 Who • 6 sad • 7 then • 8 free • 9 beaches • 10 move • 11 slow • 12 too • 13 weird • 14 bully • 15 trouble • 16 those • 17 them • 18 some

21 New words and phrases
▸ pp. 33–34 | VOCABULARY p. 243

1 him • 2 Still • 3 her • 4 his • 5 These are my friends. • 6 I'm happy that • 7 first • 8 acting • 9 loud • 10 opinion • 11 next

22 New words and phrases
▸ p. 36 | VOCABULARY pp. 248–249

1 learn; vocabulary/vocab • 2 mind map • 3 way • 4 file • 5 word • 6 from; to

23 New words and phrases
▸ p. 37 | VOCABULARY p. 249

1 make • 2 step • 3 useful • 4 before you take a photo • 5 difficult

24 Listen carefully!

1 friend • 2 They're • 3 different • 4 favourite • 5 geography • 6 difficult • 7 opinion • 8 break • 9 canteen • 10 isn't

25 Let's talk: Über Freunde/Freundinnen und den Schulalltag sprechen
▸ p. 225 and 228

This is Mia. She's ten **years old**. I'm ten (years old) **too**. We're in the **same class**. Mia is my **best friend**. She's always **helpful/nice**. The other **students** in my class are **helpful/nice** too. I'm **happy/lucky** because I'm not **alone**. I'm a **very lucky/ happy** girl.

Unit 2: My family and home

1 New words and phrases
► pp. 50–51 | VOCABULARY pp. 249–250

1 family • 2 home • 3 aunt • 4 uncle • 5 brothers • 6 sister • 7 cousin • 8 cousin • 9 daughter; son • 10 circle • 11 neighbours • 12 stepmum • 13 marry • 14 married to

2 Lost words

1 in • 2 at • 3 from • 4 for • 5 on • 6 of • 7 down

3 Family words

1 brother • 2 cousin • 3 stepdad • 4 uncle • 5 sister • 6 daughters • 7 sons • 8 aunt

4 New words and phrases
► pp. 52–53 | VOCABULARY pp. 250–251

1 pet • 2 lots of / a lot of • 3 rabbit • 4 Hamsters • 5 Are you lost? • 6 angry • 7 vet • 8 weekend; so • 9 work • 10 house • 11 messy • 12 polite • 13 only

5 New words and phrases
► p. 54 | VOCABULARY p. 251

1 homework • 2 missing • 3 fly • 4 call; when • 5 If • 6 find

6 Bits and pieces

1 daughter • 2 stepmum • 3 neighbour • 4 weekend • 5 homework • 6 polite • 7 rabbit • 8 hamster

7 New words and phrases
► p. 55 | VOCABULARY pp. 251–252

1 want • 2 active • 3 cute • 4 fast • 5 interesting • 6 special • 7 lizard • 8 quite • 9 dream

8 New words and phrases
► p. 56 | VOCABULARY p. 252

1 trees; garden • 2 ground floor • 3 top floor • 4 flat; balcony • 5 garages • 6 Each • 7 lamp • 8 no

9 New words and phrases
► p. 57 | VOCABULARY pp. 252–253

1 tour • 2 bedroom • 3 bathroom • 4 dining room • 5 kitchen • 6 living room • 7 office

10 The fourth word

1 brother • 2 daughter • 3 loud • 4 mean • 5 swim

11 Listen carefully!

1 circle • 2 active • 3 quite • 4 quiet • 5 neighbours • 6 special • 7 interesting • 8 dream

12 New words and phrases
► p. 58 | VOCABULARY p. 253

1 sunny • 2 modern • 3 live; street • 4 Tell

13 New words and phrases
► p. 59 | VOCABULARY p. 253

1 block of flats • 2 terraced home/house • 3 detached home/house • 4 semi-detached home/house • 5 their • 6 describe • 7 cottage • 8 little

14 New words and phrases
► p. 60 | VOCABULARY pp. 253–254

1 in front of • 2 mirror • 3 under • 4 shelves • 5 between • 6 chocolate • 7 wardrobe • 8 cushions • 9 chair • 10 robot • 11 behind • 12 bed • 13 over • 14 clothes • 15 table • 16 next to • 17 shelf

15 New words and phrases
► pp. 61–63 | VOCABULARY p. 254

1 door • 2 tidy • 3 person • 4 sweets • 5 its terrarium • 6 my own • 7 walls

16 New words and phrases
► p. 64 | VOCABULARY p. 255

1 expensive • 2 perfect • 3 enough • 4 problem • 5 parents • 6 Of course • 7 funny • 8 speak • 9 Speak later

17 Odd word out

1 vet • 2 dream • 3 tree • 4 cushion

18 Lost words

1 you • 2 your • 3 it • 4 our • 5 my • 6 She • 7 Her • 8 He • 9 His • 10 They • 11 Their • 12 I • 13 Its • 14 you • 15 your

19 New words and phrases
► p. 65 | VOCABULARY p. 255

1 Dinner • 2 love • 3 rude • 4 part • 5 electric • 6 headphones • 7 games • 8 back

20 What's the right word: *have* or *has*?

1 has • 2 has • 3 have • 4 has • 5 have • 6 have

21 New words and phrases
► p. 66 | VOCABULARY pp. 255–256

1 on the phone • 2 idea • 3 noise • 4 long • 5 solution

22 Opposites

1 messy • 2 passive • 3 fast • 4 under • 5 rude

23 New words and phrases
► p. 68 | VOCABULARY p. 256

1 spell • 2 alphabet • 3 address • 4 like this • 5 oh • 6 Write

24 New words and phrases
► p. 69 | VOCABULARY p. 256

1 Present • 2 photographer

25 Lost words

1 to • 2 of • 3 with • 4 at • 5 about • 6 on • 7 from; to • 8 in

26 Listen carefully!

1 fifteen • **2** fifty • **3** eighty • **4** fourteen • **5** perfect • **6** There • **7** their • **8** balcony • **9** garages • **10** garden

27 That's wrong!

1 Your uncle is your mother's **brother**. • **2** People cook their food in the **kitchen**. • **3** Rabbits **can't/cannot** fly. • **4** Lions **aren't** good pets.

28 Let's talk: Das eigene Zuhause beschreiben

▸ pp. 226–227

1 ground floor • **2** bedroom(s) • **3** first floor • **4** bathroom • **5** garage • **6** kitchen • **7** dining room • **8** balcony • **9** living room • **10** garden

(*Lösungsbeispiel*) I can see a nice/big house in the picture. There are two floors. On the ground floor, there is a living room, a dining room and a kitchen. On the first floor, there are two bedrooms and a bathroom. There is a balcony next to the parents' bedroom. In the garage, I see two bikes. There is a nice garden with two trees in front of the house.

Unit 3: My day

1 New words and phrases

▸ pp. 84–85 | VOCABULARY pp. 256–257

1 journey • **2** come • **3** bus • **4** by bike • **5** by car • **6** by train • **7** short

2 New words and phrases

▸ p. 86 | VOCABULARY p. 257

1 weekdays • **2** at 10 o'clock • **3** at 5 p.m. • **4** at 2 a.m. • **5** United Kingdom (UK) • **6** hours • **7** clock • **8** in the morning; in the evening • **9** afternoon • **10** at lunchtime • **11** end • **12** What's the time?

3 New words and phrases

▸ p. 87 | VOCABULARY pp. 257–258

1 Why • **2** newspaper • **3** letters • **4** competition • **5** best • **6** choose • **7** winner; wins • **8** illness • **9** wheelchair • **10** husband • **11** cafe • **12** get up • **13** have a shower • **14** get dressed • **15** Breakfast • **16** take • **17** watch

4 Bits and pieces

1 weekday • **2** morning • **3** journey • **4** lunchtime • **5** evening • **6** wheelchair • **7** husband • **8** newspaper

5 Lost words

1 When • **2** Why • **3** What • **4** How • **5** Where • **6** Who

6 New words and phrases

▸ pp. 88–89 | VOCABULARY pp. 258–259

1 line • **2** go shopping • **3** brush; teeth • **4** tooth • **5** Everybody • **6** project • **7** country

7 Listen carefully!

1 journey • 2 hours • 3 country • 4 United Kingdom • 5 competition

8 New words and phrases

▸ p. 90 | VOCABULARY p. 259

1 drama • 2 cycles • 3 hiking • 4 running • 5 trampolining • 6 Which • 7 join • 8 how to • 9 every • 10 month • 11 by the sea • 12 exciting

9 Lost words

1 On • 2 up • 3 at • 4 before • 5 in • 6 to • 7 at • 8 in • 9 after • 10 At • 11 in • 12 At • 13 by • 14 On • 15 to

10 New words and phrases

▸ pp. 91–93 | VOCABULARY pp. 259–260

1 sometimes • 2 never • 3 rarely • 4 feels • 5 stressed • 6 matches • 7 secret • 8 sentences

11 School clubs

1 hockey club • 2 art club • 3 hiking club • 4 trampolining club

12 New words and phrases

▸ pp. 94–96 | VOCABULARY p. 260

1 all weekend • 2 a shame • 3 I'd love to. / I would love to. • 4 asks; to do • 5 plans • 6 sound • 7 hang out

13 Letter code

1 o • 2 e • 3 a • 4 i

14 New words and phrases

▸ p. 97 | VOCABULARY pp. 260–261

1 crack • 2 popular • 3 field • 4 crickets • 5 bat • 6 ball • 7 design

15 New words and phrases

▸ p. 98 | VOCABULARY p. 261

1 prizes • 2 show • 3 her • 4 articles • 5 surprised • 6 send • 7 guys • 8 are/feel sorry for • 9 stare • 10 hate

16 What's the word?

1 often • 2 never • 3 sometimes • 4 always • 5 rarely

17 Odd word out

1 clock • 2 husband • 3 hour • 4 shopping

18 New words and phrases

▸ p. 99 | VOCABULARY pp. 261–262

1 Thank you very much • 2 Well done. • 3 text • 4 That is good/great news! / Great news! • 5 as • 6 money • 7 heading • 8 find out • 9 explain; to me • 10 happens

19 New words and phrases

▸ p. 100 | VOCABULARY p. 262

1 freeze-frames • 2 pay for • 3 cleaner • 4 bank • 5 pounds; pence

20 Opposites

1 hate • **2** weekend • **3** never • **4** short

21 Listen carefully!

1 winner; competition • **2** 7 o'clock / seven o'clock • **3** always; newspaper • **4** rarely; breakfast • **5** wheelchair • **6** choose; clubs • **7** shower; morning • **8** shopping; afternoon

22 Scrambled words

1 explain; exercise • **2** where; secret • **3** lunchtime • **4** always; before

23 New words and phrases

▸ p. 102 | VOCABULARY p. 262

1 Look; up • **2** jigsaws / jigsaw puzzles • **3** collects • **4** second • **5** cards • **6** languages • **7** group

24 New words and phrases

▸ p. 103 | VOCABULARY p. 263

1 share • **2** think about • **3** superhero • **4** task • **5** add • **6** speech bubbles • **7** record • **8** for example • **9** light • **10** speak clearly

25 Let's talk: Über den Schulalltag sprechen

▸ pp. 228–229

(*Lösungsbeispiel*) My school journey is short. Our first lesson starts at 8 a.m. I go to school by bus. Lunchtime at our school is at twelve thirty. I have lunch with my friends. I come home from school at 4 p.m. After school I do my homework. It takes an hour. I always have a lot of homework.

26 Let's talk: Über den Tagesablauf sprechen

▸ pp. 229–230

(*Lösungsbeispiel*) On weekdays I get up at 7 a.m. I have a shower, get dressed and have breakfast with my parents. Then I walk to school.
I have lunch at school. In the afternoon I do my homework.
I sometimes meet friends and play games with them. My parents work long days. They come home in the evening. Weekends are different.

Unit 4: Where I live

1 New words and phrases

▸ pp. 116–117 | VOCABULARY pp. 263–264

1 cinema • **2** pier • **3** boring • **4** busy • **5** palace • **6** Duke • **7** marina • **8** north • **9** have a picnic • **10** hear • **11** practises • **12** skills • **13** chips • **14** miles • **15** kilometres • **16** point

2 New words and phrases

▸ pp. 118–119 | VOCABULARY p. 264

1 smells • **2** cooking • **3** clean • **4** dirty • **5** youth centre • **6** field • **7** estate • **8** town • **9** into the town centre • **10** look after • **11** rubbish • **12** bins • **13** make notes

3 New words and phrases

▸ p. 120 | VOCABULARY p. 265

1 like • 2 boxing • 3 crafts • 4 girls' group • 5 what else • 6 buy

4 New words and phrases

▸ p. 121 | VOCABULARY p. 265

1 also • 2 village • 3 many • 4 much

5 Rhyme words

1 chair; near • 2 great; street • 3 now; no • 4 how; two

6 New words and phrases

▸ p. 122 | VOCABULARY pp. 265–266

1 hospital • 2 ice rink • 3 library • 4 supermarket • 5 Museums • 6 stadium • 7 (train) station • 8 biggest • 9 that

7 New words and phrases

▸ p. 123 | VOCABULARY p. 266

1 visitors • 2 another • 3 information

8 New words and phrases

▸ pp. 124–125 | VOCABULARY p. 266

1 everywhere • 2 head • 3 guide dog • 4 fish and chip shop • 5 warm • 6 get; warm • 7 summer • 8 Excuse me • 9 something • 10 Welcome to • 11 ice cream

9 New words and phrases

▸ p. 126 | VOCABULARY pp. 266–268

1 weather • 2 rainy • 3 snowy • 4 cloudy • 5 windy • 6 Russia; Russian • 7 outside • 8 I'm cold; inside • 9 woman; women • 10 up • 11 travel • 12 amazing • 13 view • 14 seconds

10 What's the word: *much* or *many*?

1 many • 2 many • 3 much • 4 many • 5 many • 6 much

11 Listen carefully!

1 practice • 2 practise • 3 busy • 4 kilometres • 5 smell; kitchen • 6 small estate • 7 girls' group; youth centre • 8 hospital; village • 9 married to • 10 fish and chip shop

12 Word search

1 plans • 2 dance • 3 loves • 4 snows • 5 answer • 6 drink • 7 phone • 8 rains • 9 help • 10 works • 11 walk • 12 cook

13 New words and phrases

▸ pp. 127–128 | VOCABULARY p. 268

1 more • 2 Stop • 3 costs • 4 upside down • 5 degrees • 6 need • 7 need to help • 8 tips • 9 Turn; over • 10 hot • 11 swap

14 New words and phrases

▸ p. 129 | VOCABULARY pp. 268–269

1 looks • 2 beautiful • 3 terrible • 4 isn't it • 5 island • 6 Bring; changes • 7 umbrella • 8 at the moment • 9 shines • 10 go up

15 New words and phrases

▸ pp. 130–132 | VOCABULARY pp. 269–270

1 clean up • **2** guess • **3** Well • **4** so (that) • **5** Over there. • **6** forget • **7** together • **8** dead • **9** mouse • **10** mice • **11** Next • **12** dig • **13** bark at • **14** wedding • **15** bags of rubbish • **16** furniture • **17** put up • **18** notice • **19** Somebody/Someone • **20** mean • **21** scenes • **22** go green • **23** toy

16 Opposites

1 hot • **2** up • **3** (to) stop • **4** summer • **5** outside • **6** dirty • **7** exciting • **8** unfriendly • **9** (to) remember • **10** over there

17 Listen carefully!

1 cloudy • **2** windy; inside • **3** cold; outside • **4** every; minutes • **5** looks; expensive • **6** women over there • **7** woman • **8** grandparents; grandsons; granddaughter

18 New words and phrases

▸ p. 134 | VOCABULARY p. 271

1 greet • **2** audience • **3** title • **4** phrase • **5** Do you have any questions? • **6** continue

19 New words and phrases

▸ p. 135 | VOCABULARY p. 271

1 zoo • **2** rides • **3** topic

20 Word partners

cycle – ride a bike, buy sth. – get sth., match – game, little – small, grandparents – your parents' parents, kind – friendly, old – not new

21 Secret sentence

1 cooking • **2** palace • **3** stadium • **4** visitors • **5** weather • **6** rink • **7** buy • **8** barks • **9** youth • **10** rubbish • **11** library • **Secret sentence:** I am very busy.

22 Let's talk: Über den Wohnort und die Nachbarschaft sprechen

▸ p. 227

(*Lösungsbeispiel*) **Where I live and what I can do there**
I live in ***[dein Wohnort]***. That's a big/small **village/town/city** in **Germany**.
We live in a **flat/house** / on an **estate** / by **the sea** / in the **country**.
My neighbourhood is **very quiet/busy/nice**. / My neighbourhood has **some problems**.
There is a **park/zoo in my village/town**. There are **schools and shops in my village/town**.
There isn't a **cinema** and there aren't any **youth clubs**.
I like living here because **I have lots of friends and my grandparents live here too**.

23 Let's talk: Feedback geben

▸ p. 231

(*Lösungsbeispiel*) **1** Please speak (more) loudly. • **2** Don't speak so fast, please. • **3** Please look at us. • **4** That was useful information. • **5** Your presentation is/was cool / very nice. • **6** Well done! / Great job!.

1 New words and phrases

► pp. 148–149 | VOCABULARY pp. 271–273

1 enjoys • 2 desserts • 3 birthday • 4 Christmas • 5 fruit • 6 jelly • 7 strawberries; cream • 8 allergic to • 9 Indian restaurant • 10 dishes • 11 meat • 12 vegetarian • 13 cheese • 14 peas • 15 tomatoes • 16 spices • 17 usually • 18 bread • 19 Rice • 20 vegetables • 21 recipe • 22 health • 23 For this reason • 24 religious

2 New words and phrases

► pp. 150–151 | VOCABULARY p. 273

1 invitation • 2 sausages • 3 cake • 4 twelfth (12th) birthday • 5 circus • 6 by phone • 7 season • 8 date • 9 on 1st April (*gesprochen:* on the first of April)

3 Letter code

1 s • 2 i • 3 a • 4 o

4 New words and phrases

► pp. 152–153 | VOCABULARY p. 273

1 rest • 2 juggle • 3 sleeps • 4 must • 5 teach • 6 lies • 7 balloons

5 Months

1 April • 2 December • 3 March • 4 October • 5 July • 6 February • 7 August • 8 January • 9 May • 10 September • 11 November • 12 June

6 New words and phrases

► p. 154 | VOCABULARY p. 274

1 presents • 2 magic set • 3 What about a • 4 sure • 5 already

7 Nouns and adjectives

1 healthy • 2 spicy • 3 cloudy • 4 British; German • 5 funny • 6 sunny

8 New words and phrases

► pp. 155–156 | VOCABULARY pp. 274–275

1 kind • 2 salad • 3 piece • 4 shopping list • 5 packet • 6 ham • 7 melon • 8 sugar • 9 menu • 10 carrots • 11 lemonade • 12 lemon

9 Listen carefully!

1 twenty-ninth; May • 2 invitation; party • 3 Saturday; third; June • 4 present • 5 buy; circus • 6 great; Why don't we; together • 7 I'm not sure; expensive • 8 another idea • 9 cycling; bike lights • 10 See you soon

10 Odd word out

1 dessert • 2 salad • 3 Christmas • 4 rice • 5 (to) wear • 6 jelly

11 Word search

Die neun Verben: rest, enjoy, teach, sleep, sit, wear, stand, lie, juggle
Im Text: 1 enjoying • 2 sitting • 3 juggle • 4 sleep • 5 teach • 6 wearing

12 New words and phrases

▸ p. 158 | VOCABULARY pp. 275–276

1 grams (g) • 2 flour • 3 millilitres (ml) • 4 oil • 5 cocoa • 6 milk • 7 eggs • 8 salt • 9 teaspoon • 10 vanilla • 11 baking powder • 12 icing • 13 butter • 14 mixture • 15 oven • 16 break • 17 decorate

13 Bits and pieces

1 millilitre • 2 sausage • 3 difference • 4 teaspoon • 5 vanilla • 6 mixture • 7 balloon • 8 present

14 New words and phrases

▸ p. 159 | VOCABULARY p. 276

1 like better • 2 false • 3 true • 4 fry • 5 savoury • 6 scone • 7 round • 8 jam • 9 chicken • 10 tastes

15 New words and phrases

▸ p. 160 | VOCABULARY pp. 276–277

1 main course • 2 's/is; called • 3 Nigeria; Nigerians • 4 onions • 5 pepper(s) • 6 delicious • 7 Bananas • 8 honey • 9 important • 10 culture • 11 tradition • 12 Chinese; China • 13 stir-fry • 14 noodles • 15 tea; coffee

16 Lost words

1 of • 2 on • 3 to • 4 on; of • 5 at • 6 up • 7 to • 8 about • 9 of • 10 of • 11 for

17 New words and phrases

▸ p. 161 | VOCABULARY pp. 277–278

1 Afternoon tea; meal • 2 preheat • 3 rolling out; dough • 4 glass • 5 cut • 6 potatoes • 7 crumbs • 8 garlic

18 New words and phrases

▸ pp. 162–163 | VOCABULARY p. 278

1 waving • 2 is; good at it • 3 just • 4 a little • 5 Don't worry • 6 faces • 7 smiles • 8 it's; turn

19 Different sounds

1 <u>big</u>; mice; nice • 2 <u>have</u>; brave; hate • 3 <u>glue</u>; come; run • 4 <u>how</u>; show; slow • 5 <u>head</u>; me, sweet

20 New words and phrases

▸ p. 167 | VOCABULARY p. 279

1 researching • 2 boil • 3 introduction • 4 instructions

21 Listen carefully!

1 cook; Indian restaurant • 2 delicious dishes • 3 vegetarian meals • 4 baking • 5 bakes; birthday cake • 6 recipe book • 7 sweet • 8 sugar; honey; tea • 9 vegan; eggs; cream • 10 kinds of; coffee

22 Singulars and plurals

1 one tomato • 2 five children • 3 two buses • 4 one child • 5 three ponies • 6 four women • 7 one fish • 8 one pony • 9 three fish • 10 one woman • 11 six tomatoes • 12 one bus

23 Let's talk: Über den Tagesablauf sprechen, sich verabreden

▸ pp. 229–230

(*Lösungsbeispiel*) **1** What do you usually do at the weekend? • **2** What are you doing at the moment? • **3** Where's the party? • **4** Thanks for the invitation. • **5** Send me a message if you can come or not.

24 Let's talk: Über Essen und Lebensmittel sprechen

▸ p. 231

(*Lösungsbeispiel*) We eat a lot of fruit and vegetables. • We like vegetarian food because it's healthy. • My sister is a vegan. • My parents eat meat. • I'm allergic to apples. • Our favourite dish is pizza. / Our favourite dishes are Indian meals with lots of spices. • What food do you eat?

°Unit 6: The lost dog

1 New words and phrases

▸ pp. 182–183 | VOCABULARY pp. 279–280

1 bottle • **2** smooth • **3** cloudy • **4** rocks • **5** several • **6** colourful • **7** is crying • **8** Poor • **9** owner • **10** I'm glad • **11** is collecting • **12** child • **13** children • **14** hope • **15** animal shelter • **16** keep • **17** a few • **18** whisper • **19** follow • **20** laugh at • **21** licking • **22** leave

2 New words and phrases

▸ p. 184 | VOCABULARY p. 280

1 diary • **2** was • **3** came • **4** Yesterday • **5** played • **6** had • **7** tomorrow • **8** kick • **9** runs for • **10** What's wrong? • **11** saw • **12** looking for

3 Bits and pieces

1 bottle • **2** follow • **3** whisper • **4** colourful • **5** collect • **6** children • **7** several • **8** tomorrow

4 New words and phrases

▸ pp. 185–187 | VOCABULARY pp. 280–281

1 tears • **2** kisses • **3** doorbell • **4** Come in • **5** wags; tail • **6** granddaughters • **7** age • **8** about • **9** strong • **10** hug • **11** wonderful • **12** gave • **13** tonight

5 New words and phrases

▸ pp. 188–189 | VOCABULARY p. 281

1 tall • **2** hair • **3** through • **4** police • **5** pocket • **6** fall down • **7** policewoman • **8** policewomen • **9** run over • **10** police officer • **11** police officer • **12** out of • **13** found • **14** past

6 Missing words

1 hug • **2** leave • **3** cries • **4** kick • **5** hope • **6** keep

7 Lost words

1 at • **2** of • **3** for • **4** with • **5** for • **6** down • **7** out • **8** at • **9** to

8 Scrambled words

1 several; animal shelter • **2** Children; colourful • **3** Yesterday; policewomen • **4** theatre; tonight • **5** granddaughter; police officer • **6** police; looking

9 Different sounds

1 through; loud, mouse • **2** brush; new, room • **3** old; block, sock • **4** fish; eye, time • **5** like; if, kiss

10 Opposites

1 (to) sit down • **2** out of • **3** a few • **4** false • **5** savoury food • **6** wonderful • **7** cloudy/rainy • **8** (to) keep

11 Word search

Im Wortgitter: **1** play • **2** find • **3** see • **4** give • **5** be • **6** come • **7** have

1 ... the weather was horrible.
2 Grandpa and Grandma came to see us.
3 We had a great time together.
4 We played lots of games.
5 Grandma gave me some money for a new blazer.
6 Grandma and Grandpa saw my new bedroom.
7 I found my mobile under my bed.

12 Right or wrong?

Right: **2** and **4**
Wrong: **1** and **3**
1 "Wonderful" means "very good", "great".
3 A granddaughter is your child's daughter.

13 Secret sentence

1 age • **2** hair • **3** leave • **4** tall • **5** about • **6** jam • **7** pockets • **8** bottle • **9** owner • **10** Poor • **11** strong • **12** wonderful • **13** came • **14** glad • **15** saw • **16** past • **17** few • **18** diary

Secret sentence: Great job, wordmaster!

10 New words and phrases

▸ pp. 91–93 | VOCABULARY pp. 259–260

1 Mum _____ works from home.	Mama arbeitet **manchmal** von zu Hause.
2 Dad _____ cycles to work.	Papa fährt **nie** mit dem Rad zur Arbeit.
3 I _____ take the bus to school.	Ich fahre **selten** mit dem Bus zur Schule.
4 Today Sam _____ sad.	Heute **fühlt** sich Sam traurig.
5 He is very _____ with his work.	Er ist sehr **gestresst** mit seiner Arbeit.
6 I play football in a club and my parents watch all our _____.	Ich spiele Fußball im Verein und meine Eltern schauen sich alle unsere **Spiele** an.
7 "What's wrong with her?" – "Sorry, I can't tell you, it's a _____."	„Was stimmt mit ihr nicht? – „Tut mir leid, das kann ich dir nicht sagen, es ist ein **Geheimnis**."
8 Write six _____ about your club.	Schreibe sechs **Sätze** über deine AG.

11 School clubs

Sieh dir die Bilder an. Für welche AG stehen sie jeweils? Schreibe den englischen Begriff auf.

1

hockey club

2

_____

3

_____

4

_____

12 New words and phrases

▸ pp. 94–96 | VOCABULARY p. 260

1 Sam is busy _____.	Sam ist **das ganze Wochenende** beschäftigt.
2 "I can't come to your party." – "What _____!"	„Ich kann nicht zu deiner Party kommen." „Wie **schade**!"
3 "Would you like to play tennis with me this afternoon?" – "_____."	„Möchtest du heute Nachmittag Tennis mit mir spielen?" – „**Sehr gerne.**"
4 My father sometimes _____ me _____ the shopping for him.	Mein Vater **bittet** mich manchmal, die Einkäufe für ihn **zu erledigen**.
5 What are your _____ for Sunday?	Was sind deine **Pläne** für Sonntag?
6 You _____ like your sister.	Du **klingst** wie deine Schwester.
7 My brother and I often _____ in our garden.	Mein Bruder und ich **hängen** oft in unserem Garten **ab**.

13 Letter code

Welche Buchstaben sind 1, 2, 3 und 4?

1 Wh3t's y1ur f3v1ur4t2 3ct4v4ty?

2 4 l4k2 h4k4ng 4n th2 c1untry.

3 4 c3n't g1 t1 th2 t3bl2 t2nn4s club th4s 3ft2rn11n.

1: ______ 2: ______ 3: ______ 4: ______

14 New words and phrases

▸ p. 97 | VOCABULARY pp. 260–261

1 Can you help me? I can't ______________ this problem.	Kannst du mir helfen? Ich kann dieses Problem nicht **lösen**.
2 Ms Black is a very ______________ teacher.	Frau Black ist eine sehr **beliebte** Lehrerin.
3 Is there a sports ______________ near your house?	Gibt es einen Sport**platz** in der Nähe deines Hauses?
4 I like the sound of ______________.	Ich mag den Klang der **Grillen**.
5 Is your baseball ______________ new?	Ist dein Baseball**schläger** neu?
6 Let's play with your new ______________.	Lass uns mit deinem neuen **Ball** spielen.
7 I ______________ all my clothes.	Ich **entwerfe** meine gesamte Kleidung.

15 New words and phrases

▸ p. 98 | VOCABULARY p. 261

1 There are some great ______________ for the winners.	Es gibt tolle **Preise** für die Gewinner.
2 Can you ______________ me a photo of your dog?	Kannst du mir ein Foto von deinem Hund **zeigen**?
3 Where is Cara? I can't see ______________.	Wo ist Cara? Ich kann **sie** nicht sehen.
4 Rishi writes ______________ for different newspapers.	Rishi schreibt **Artikel** für verschiedene Zeitungen.
5 John is really ______________ when he wins the first prize.	John ist sehr **überrascht**, als er den ersten Preis gewinnt.
6 Please ______________ me your address.	Bitte **schicke** mir deine Adresse.
7 Hey ______________, what's that noise?	Hey, **Leute**, was ist das für ein Lärm?
8 His friends ______________ him.	Seine Freunde **haben Mitleid mit** ihm.
9 Please don't ______________ at the old man.	Bitte **starre** den alten Mann nicht an.
10 I ______________ bad food.	Ich **hasse** schlechtes Essen.

16 What's the word?

Vervollständige die Sätze mit den Wörtern aus dem Kasten.

always • never • often • rarely • sometimes

1 Sina really likes sport, so she ____________ plays football or tennis in the afternoon.
2 Hien's school journey is very long, so he ____________ cycles to school but takes the bus.
3 Mum loves cooking and ____________ my brother and I help her with it.
4 Lara loves maths, so she ____________ does her maths homework.
5 Today, people send messages on their phones.
They ____________ write letters.

17 Odd word out

Unterstreiche das Wort, das nicht in die Reihe passt.

1 bus – car – train – clock
2 sister – husband – daughter – mother
3 hour – dinner – lunch – breakfast
4 afternoon – morning – evening – shopping

18 New words and phrases

▸ p. 99 | VOCABULARY pp. 261–262

1	____________ for your help!	**Vielen Dank** für Ihre Hilfe!
2	Here's your prize, Lara! ____________.	Hier ist dein Preis, Lara! **Gut gemacht.**
3	Please ____________ me if you're late.	Bitte **schick** mir **eine SMS**, wenn du dich verspätest.
4	"Lara can go to school again." – "____________!"	„Lara kann wieder zur Schule gehen." – „**Das sind gute Nachrichten!**"
5	He works ____________ a teacher.	Er arbeitet **als** Lehrer.
6	Mum, can I have some ____________?	Mama, kann ich etwas **Geld** haben?
7	Find a good ____________ for your story.	Finde eine gute **Überschrift** für deine Geschichte.
8	Can you ____________ where John lives?	Kannst du **herausfinden**, wo John wohnt?
9	Can you ____________ this exercise ____________?	Kannst du **mir** diese Aufgabe **erklären**?
10	What ____________ in the film?	Was **passiert** in dem Film?

19 New words and phrases

▸ p. 100 | VOCABULARY p. 262

1 Present the text in _______________.	Stellt den Text in **Standbildern** dar.
2 Let me _______________ the food.	Lass mich das Essen **bezahlen**.
3 Ron works as a _______________.	Ron arbeitet als **Reinigungskraft**.
4 Lara's mother works in a _______________.	Laras Mutter arbeitet bei einer **Bank**.
5 The book is eight _______________ and fifty _______________.	Das Buch kostet acht **Pfund** und fünfzig **Pence**.

20 Opposites

Finde die Gegenteile.

1 (to) love ◂▸ _______________

2 weekdays ◂▸ _______________

3 always ◂▸ _______________

4 long ◂▸ _______________

21 Listen carefully!

07

Höre dir die Sätze aufmerksam an und schreibe die fehlenden Wörter in die Lücken.

1 Who is the _______________ of the art _______________?

2 On weekdays, I get up at _______________.

3 My parents _______________ read the _______________ in the morning.

4 Mr Cox _______________ has _______________ on weekdays.

5 My brother uses a _______________.

6 Please _______________ two school _______________.

7 Sina has a _______________ each _______________.

8 Can we go _______________ in the _______________?

22 Scrambled words

Hier sind einige Buchstaben durcheinandergeraten. Schreibe die Wörter richtig auf.

1 Please *plaexin* this *eercexis* to me. _______________

2 I can't tell you *erwhe* he lives. It's a *crseet*. _______________

3 Can we meet at *menchtlui*? _______________

4 Sina *waalys* plays with her cat *orbeef* school. _______________

23 New words and phrases

▶ p. 102 | VOCABULARY p. 262

1	"What's 'guys' in German?" – "__________ it __________ in a dictionary."	„Wie heißt ‚guys' auf Deutsch?" – „**Schlage** es in einem Wörterbuch **nach**."
2	Most kids like __________.	Die meisten Kinder mögen **Puzzle**.
3	Jake __________ old phones.	Jake **sammelt** alte Telefone.
4	What's the __________ letter of your name.	Was ist der **zweite** Buchstabe deines Namens?
5	Zoe has lots of animal __________.	Zoe hat viele Tier**karten**.
6	Hien speaks four __________.	Hien spricht vier **Sprachen**.
7	Max likes working in a __________.	Max arbeitet gern in einer **Gruppe**.

24 New words and phrases

▶ p. 103 | VOCABULARY p. 263

1	Julia and her sister __________ a room.	Julia und ihre Schwester **teilen sich** ein Zimmer.
2	Let's __________ a name for our new dog.	Lass uns **über** einen Namen für unseren neuen Hund **nachdenken**.
3	My brother is my __________. He is always there for me.	Mein Bruder ist mein **Superheld**. Er ist immer für mich da.
4	Please do __________ 4 now.	Bitte bearbeitet jetzt **Aufgabe** 4.
5	You can __________ photos to your text.	Du kannst Fotos zu deinem Text **hinzufügen**.
6	Draw a comic with __________.	Zeichne einen Comic mit **Sprechblasen**.
7	I sometimes __________ messages for my mother.	Ich **nehme** manchmal Sprachnachrichten für meine Mutter **auf**.
8	Bring two favourite things to school, __________ __________ a book and a CD.	Bring zwei Lieblingsdinge mit zur Schule, **zum Beispiel** ein Buch und eine CD.
9	I have no __________ on my bike.	Ich habe kein **Licht** an meinem Fahrrad.
10	Please __________.	Bitte **sprich deutlich**.

25 Let's talk: Über den Schulalltag sprechen

▸ pp. 228–229

Vervollständige zunächst die Mindmap. Beschreibe dann einer englischen Freundin / einem englischen Freund deinen Schulalltag. Du kannst deine Beschreibung auch aufnehmen und jemanden bitten, sie sich anzuhören und dir Feedback zu geben.

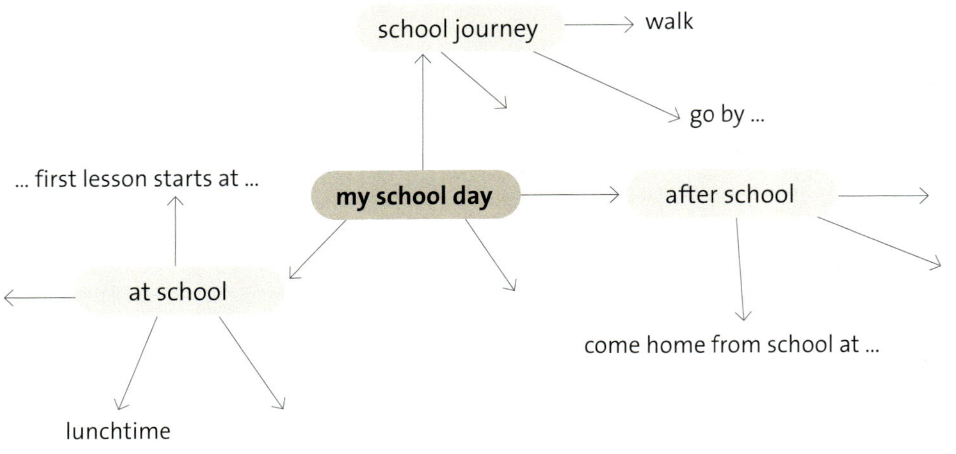

Our first lesson starts at ...

26 Let's talk: Über den Tagesablauf sprechen

▸ pp. 229–230

Beschreibe nun einer englischen Freundin / einem englischen Freund deinen Tagesablauf. Die Wörter in dem Kasten helfen dir. Du kannst deine Beschreibung auch aufnehmen und jemanden bitten, sie sich anzuhören und dir Feedback zu geben.

afternoon • at • breakfast • different • evening • friends • (to) get dressed • (to) get up • homework • in • lunch • (to) meet • parents • (to) play • school • shower • walk • weekdays • weekends • (to) work

On weekdays, I get up at ...

Unit 4
Where I live

1 New words and phrases

► pp. 116–117 | VOCABULARY pp. 263–264

1 There is a good ______________ near our house where I often watch films.	In der Nähe unseres Hauses gibt es ein gutes **Kino**, in dem ich mir oft Filme anschaue.
2 Can you see the seagulls on the ______________?	Siehst du die Möwen auf der **Seebrücke**?
3 Homework is sometimes ______________.	Hausaufgaben sind manchmal **langweilig**.
4 The beach is very ______________ on Sundays.	Sonntags ist der Strand sehr **belebt**.
5 A ______________ is a nice, big building.	Ein **Palast** ist ein schönes, großes Gebäude.
6 Queen Elizabeth's husband was the ______________ of Edinburgh.	Königin Elizabeths Ehemann war der **Herzog** von Edinburgh.
7 Brighton has a nice ______________.	Brighton hat einen schönen **Jachthafen**.
8 I live in the ______________ of England.	Ich lebe im **Norden** Englands.
9 When we go hiking, we always ______________ ______________.	Wenn wir wandern gehen, **machen** wir immer **ein Picknick**.
10 Can you ______________ me?	Kannst du mich **hören**?
11 Lara ______________ the piano every day.	Lara **übt** jeden Tag Klavier.
12 She wants to learn new ______________.	Sie möchte neue **Fertigkeiten** erlernen.
13 Dunja loves fish and ______________.	Dunja liebt Fisch und **Pommes frites**.
14 Rishi runs five ______________ every day.	Rishi läuft täglich fünf **Meilen**.
15 Sina's school is three ______________ from her home.	Sinas Schule liegt drei **Kilometer** von ihrem Haus entfernt.
16 Tom lives two ______________ five km from us.	Tom wohnt zwei **Komma** fünf km von uns entfernt.

2 New words and phrases

► pp. 118–119 | VOCABULARY p. 264

1	The food ________________ nice!	Das Essen **riecht** gut!
2	Sina's favourite hobby is ________________.	Sinas liebstes Hobby ist **Kochen**.
3	I like a ________________ kitchen.	Ich mag eine **saubere** Küche.
4	Put your ________________ clothes in the bathroom.	Lege deine **schmutzige** Kleidung ins Bad.
5	Mandy goes dancing at the ________________ ________________ on Saturday evenings.	Mandy tanzt samstagabends im **Jugendzentrum**.
6	Can you see the horses in the ________________?	Siehst du die Pferde auf der **Weide**?
7	Luca lives on a small ________________.	Luca wohnt in einer kleinen **Wohnsiedlung**.
8	Brighton is a nice ________________ by the sea.	Brighton ist eine schöne **Stadt** am Meer.
9	We can walk ________________.	Wir können **ins Stadtzentrum** laufen.
10	Can you ________________ Alfie today?	Kannst du dich heute **um** Alfie **kümmern**?
11	Don't put your ________________ here.	Legen Sie Ihren **Abfall** nicht hier hin.
12	We have three different ________________.	Wir haben drei verschiedene **Mülleimer**.
13	Before you give a presentation, you can ________________.	Bevor du eine Präsentation hältst, kannst du dir **Notizen machen**.

3 New words and phrases

► p. 120 | VOCABULARY p. 265

1	Sina likes sports ________________ tennis, dancing or swimming.	Sina mag Sportarten **wie zum Beispiel** Tennis, Tanzen oder Schwimmen.
2	Lola's favourite sport is ________________.	Lolas Lieblingssportart ist **Boxen**.
3	Ben goes to the ________________ club.	Ben geht in den **Bastel**club.
4	Sina and Lola go to a ________________ ________________ at the youth centre.	Sina und Lola gehen zu einer **Mädchengruppe** in einem Jugendzentrum.
5	A sandwich and a drink – ________________ can I get you?	Ein Sandwich und ein Getränk – **was** kann ich dir **sonst noch** bringen?
6	Mum, can we ________________ some sweets?	Mama, können wir Süßigkeiten **kaufen**?

4 New words and phrases

▸ p. 121 | VOCABULARY p. 265

1 Molly likes dancing and she ________________ likes skateboarding.	Molly tanzt gern und fährt **auch gern** Skateboard.
2 Rula lives in a ________________ near London.	Rula wohnt in einem **Dorf** nahe London.
3 There aren't ________________ shops there.	Es gibt dort nicht **viele** Geschäfte.
4 I have too ________________ work to help you.	Ich habe zu **viel** Arbeit, um dir zu helfen.

5 Rhyme words

Unterstreiche in jeder Zeile das Wort, das sich nicht mit den anderen drei Wörtern reimt. Finde nun für jede Zeile ein Wort im Kasten, das sich mit den anderen drei Wörtern reimt.

near • no • street • two

1 hear pier chair here ________________

2 eat sweet meet great ________________

3 now know go show ________________

4 too who how blue ________________

6 New words and phrases

▸ p. 122 | VOCABULARY pp. 265–266

1 Tom is ill, so he's in ________________.	Tom ist krank und daher im **Krankenhaus**.
2 In winter, we often go to the ________________.	Im Winter gehen wir oft zur **Schlittschuhbahn**.
3 Lola gets lots of books from the ________________.	Lola holt sich viele Bücher aus der **Bücherei**.
4 Tom works in a ________________.	Tom arbeitet in einem **Supermarkt**.
5 ________________ are very interesting places.	**Museen** sind sehr interessante Orte.
6 I like our big ________________.	Ich mag unser großes **Stadion**.
7 Can we meet at the ________________?	Können wir uns am **Bahnhof** treffen?
8 London is the ________________ city in the UK.	London ist die **größte** Stadt im Vereinigten Königreich.
9 Tell me three songs ________________ you really like.	Nenne mir drei Lieder, **die** du wirklich gern magst.

7 New words and phrases

► p. 123 | VOCABULARY p. 266

1	We love having ____________________.	Wir haben gerne **Gäste**.
2	These sandwiches are nice. Can I have ____________________ sandwich?	Diese Sandwiches sind gut. Kann ich **noch ein** Sandwich haben?
3	Let's collect some ____________________ on the new game.	Lass uns ein paar **Informationen** über das neue Spiel sammeln.

8 New words and phrases

► pp. 124–125 | VOCABULARY p. 266

1	On the pier, there are seagulls ____________________.	**Überall** auf dem Pier sind Möwen.
2	Our class teacher has all our names in her ____________________.	Unsere Klassenlehrerin hat alle unsere Namen im **Kopf**.
3	Elana has a ____________________ to help her find her way.	Elana hat einen **Blindenhund**, der ihr hilft, den Weg zu finden.
4	Tom's parents have a ____________________ ____________________.	Toms Eltern haben eine **Imbissstube, die Fisch mit Pommes frites verkauft**.
5	On a ____________________ day we often go to the beach.	An einem **warmen** Tag gehen wir oft zum Strand.
6	In August, it can ____________ very ____________ in Germany.	Im August kann es in Deutschland sehr **warm werden**.
7	The beach is very busy in ____________________.	Im **Sommer** ist der Strand sehr belebt.
8	____________________, can you tell me the way to the stadium?	**Entschuldigen Sie**, können Sie mir den Weg zum Stadion erklären?
9	I think there is ____________________ wrong with my bike.	Ich glaube, mit meinem Fahrrad stimmt **etwas** nicht.
10	____________________ your new school!	**Willkommen an** deiner neuer Schule!
11	Would you like an ____________________?	Möchtest du ein **Eis**?

9 New words and phrases

► p. 126 | VOCABULARY pp. 266–268

1 What's the ______ like in Brighton?	Wie ist das **Wetter** in Brighton?
2 On ______ days I go to the library.	An **regnerischen** Tagen gehe ich in die Bücherei.
3 I like the ______ fields in winter.	Ich mag die **schneebedeckten** Felder im Winter.
4 It's ______ today, but there's no rain.	Es ist heute **wolkig**, aber es gibt keinen Regen.
5 Be careful with your bike. It's very ______ today.	Sei vorsichtig mit deinem Fahrrad. Es ist heute sehr **windig**.
6 Maxim is from ______. He speaks German and ______.	Maxim stammt aus **Russland**. Er spricht Deutsch und **Russisch**.
7 When the weather is good, Tom and Sina play ______.	Wenn das Wetter gut ist, spielen Tom und Sina **draußen**.
8 ______. I'd like to go ______.	**Ich friere.** Ich würde gerne nach **drinnen** gehen.
9 The ______ on the bike is Tom's mum, the ______ in the car are his grandma and his Aunt Julia.	Die **Frau** auf dem Fahrrad ist Toms Mama, die **Frauen** im Auto sind seine Oma und seine Tante Julia.
10 Don't take food ______ to your room.	Nimm kein Essen mit **hinauf** in dein Zimmer.
11 We always ______ by train.	Wir **reisen** immer mit der Bahn.
12 Your garden is ______!	Dein Garten ist **großartig**!
13 You have a great ______ from your room.	Du hast eine tolle **Aussicht** aus deinem Zimmer.
14 There are 60 ______ in a minute.	Eine Minute hat 60 **Sekunden**.

10 What's the word: *much* or *many*?

Vervollständige die Sätze mit *much* oder *many*.

1 How ______ students are in your class?
2 There aren't ______ youth centres in my town.
3 How ______ money do you have?
4 Don't eat too ______ sweets. They aren't good for you.
5 Don't ask too ______ people to come to your party. Our flat isn't very big.
6 How ______ information do you need?

11 Listen carefully!

08

Höre dir die Sätze aufmerksam an und schreibe die fehlenden Wörter in die Lücken.

1 What time is band ______________________?
2 Sina wants to ______________________ new skateboarding skills.
3 The beach is very ______________________ today.
4 Jay's school journey is five ______________________.
5 There's a funny ______________________ in the ______________________.
6 Rani lives on a ______________________ ______________________.
7 I go to a ______________________ at our ______________________.
8 Is there a ______________________ in your ______________________?
9 Luana is ______________________ ______________________ Leroy.
10 They have a ______________________.

12 Word search ↓ → ↗ ↙ ↘

Finde zwölf Wörter (Verben und Nomen) im Buchstabengitter und kreise sie ein. Vervollständige dann die Sätze mit ihnen. Achte darauf, ob du ein Verb oder ein Nomen im Satz benötigst. Möglicherweise musst du ein -s für die dritte Person Singular oder ein Plural-s ergänzen.

D	A	N	C	E	X	P	W	I
S	N	O	W	Q	E	A	O	P
R	S	C	M	V	L	P	R	H
M	W	N	O	K	S	L	K	O
H	E	L	P	O	R	A	I	N
D	R	I	N	K	K	N	M	E

1 What are your ______________ for Monday?
2 Can we ______________ at your party?
3 Our dog ______________ snow.
4 When it ______________, we always play outside.
5 Do you know the ______________ to my question?
6 Would you like a ______________?
7 Please ______________ me when you're home.
8 When it ______________, I don't go outside.
9 How can I ______________ you?
10 Mum often ______________ long hours.
11 Tom lives a short ______________ from here.
12 Dad is a great ______________. He likes food.

13 New words and phrases

▸ pp. 127–128 | VOCABULARY p. 268

1	I have some ____________ questions.	Ich habe ein paar **weitere** Fragen.
2	____________ that noise, please.	**Hört** bitte **mit** dem Lärm **auf**.
3	This car ____________ a lot of money.	Dieses Auto **kostet** viel Geld.
4	The picture looks funny. Is it ____________ ____________?	Das Bild sieht lustig aus. Ist es **verkehrt herum**?
5	It's warm today – 24 ____________.	Es ist warm heute – **24 Grad**.
6	We ____________ more time.	Wir **brauchen** mehr Zeit.
7	I can't come to your party. I ____________ ____________ my parents at the weekend.	Ich kann nicht zu deiner Party kommen. Ich **muss** am Wochenende meinen Eltern **helfen**.
8	I need some ____________ for our holiday in Rome.	Ich brauche **Tipps** für unseren Romurlaub.
9	____________ your picture ____________.	**Dreh** dein Bild **um**.
10	I'd like a ____________ drink.	Ich hätte gern ein **heißes** Getränk.
11	In the holidays we sometimes ____________ our house with our friends' house in Rome.	In den Ferien **tauschen** wir manchmal unser Haus mit dem Haus unserer Freunde in Rom.

14 New words and phrases

▸ p. 129 | VOCABULARY pp. 268-269

1	Your house ____________ very nice.	Euer Haus **sieht** sehr schön **aus**.
2	What a ____________ day! Let's go to the beach.	Was für ein **wunderschöner** Tag! Lasst uns zum Strand gehen.
3	"Lara's dog is missing." – "That's ____________ news."	„Laras Hund wird vermisst." – „Das ist ja eine **schreckliche** Nachricht."
4	This beach is nice, ____________?	Dieser Strand ist schön, **nicht wahr**?
5	Great Britain is an ____________.	Großbritannien ist eine **Insel**.
6	____________ warm clothes. The weather often ____________.	**Bring** dir warme Kleidung **mit**. Das Wetter **ändert sich** oft.
7	I like your ____________.	Dein **Regenschirm** gefällt mir.
8	I'm not at home ____________.	Ich bin **im Moment** nicht zu Hause.
9	I always clean my bike till it ____________.	Ich putze mein Fahrrad immer, bis es **glänzt**.
10	What time does the sun ____________ at the moment?	Um wie viel Uhr **geht** die Sonne zurzeit **auf**?

15 New words and phrases

▸ pp. 130–132 | VOCABULARY pp. 269–270

1	Tom needs to ________________ his room.	Tom muss sein Zimmer **sauber machen**.
2	I ________________ I can't come to party. I have too much work to do.	Ich **glaube**, dass ich nicht zu deiner Party kommen kann. Ich habe zu viel Arbeit zu erledigen.
3	Swimming in the sea in November? ____________, I'm not sure if that's a good idea.	Im November im Meer baden? **Also**, ich bin nicht sicher, ob das eine gute Idee ist.
4	Ria brings two sandwiches, ________________ she can share with Lara.	Ria hat zwei Sandwiches, **sodass** sie mit Lara teilen kann.
5	"Where is Logan?" – "________________."	„Wo ist Logan?" – „**Dort drüben.**"
6	I often ________________ my phone at home.	Ich **vergesse** oft mein Handy zu Hause.
7	We can help Grandma ________________.	Wir können Oma **zusammen** helfen.
8	There's a ________________ seagull on the beach.	Auf dem Strand ist eine **tote** Möwe.
9	Can you see the little ________________ over there?	Siehst du die kleine **Maus** da drüben?
10	Cats eat ________________.	Katzen fressen **Mäuse**.
11	________________ I'd like to go to London.	**Als Nächstes** möchte ich gern nach London fahren.
12	Don't let your dog ________________ here!	Lassen Sie Ihren Hund nicht hier **graben**!
13	Sometimes dogs ________________ people.	Manchmal **bellen** Hunde Leute **an**.
14	These are our ________________ photos.	Das sind unsere **Hochzeit**sfotos.
15	There are often ________________ in front or our house. Who puts them there?	Vor unserem Haus stehen oft **Tüten voller Müll**. Wer stellt sie dort hin?
16	Is all your ________________ new?	Sind alle eure **Möbel** neu?
17	You can ________________ some photos in your room.	Du kannst Fotos in deinem Zimmer **aufhängen**.
18	There's a ________________ at our supermarket: They need people to clean the shop.	In unserem Supermarkt hängt ein **Anschlag**: Sie brauchen Leute, die den Laden putzen.
19	Grandpa is over 90. ________________ needs to come and help him.	Opa ist über 90. **Jemand** muss kommen und ihm helfen.
20	What does "AI" ________________?	Was **bedeutet** „AI"?
21	Matt plays in all three ________________ of our school play.	Matt spielt in allen drei **Szenen** unseres Schultheaterstücks.
22	Our school wants to ________________.	Unsere Schule möchte **grün werden**.
23	Zoe loves her little ____________ elephant.	Zoe liebt ihren kleinen **Spielzeug**elefanten.

16 Opposites

Finde die Gegenteile.

1 cold ◄► ______
2 down ◄► ______
3 (to) start ◄► ______
4 winter ◄► ______
5 inside ◄► ______
6 clean ◄► ______
7 boring ◄► ______
8 friendly ◄► ______
9 (to) forget ◄► ______
10 over here ◄► ______

17 Listen carefully!

09

Höre dir die Sätze aufmerksam an und schreibe die fehlenden Wörter in die Lücken.

1 It's very ______ today.
2 When it's very ______, we always play ______.
3 I think it's too ______ today to play ______.
4 There is a train ______ 30 ______.
5 Your bike ______ very ______.
6 Who are the three ______ ______ ______?
7 Mrs Berry is a very kind ______.
8 Jay's ______ have five ______ and one ______.

18 New words and phrases

► p. 134 | VOCABULARY p. 271

1 Let's go and ______ Aunt Ava.	Lasst uns Tante Ava **begrüßen** gehen.
2 Look at your ______ when you give a presentation.	Schau dein **Publikum** an, wenn du ein Referat hältst.
3 Your story needs a good ______.	Deine Geschichte braucht einen guten **Titel**.
4 "You're welcome" is a ______ that you can use when someone says "Thank you".	„You're welcome" ist ein **Ausdruck**, den du verwenden kannst, wenn jemand „Thank you" sagt.
5 ______?	**Habt ihr / Hast du (irgendwelche) Fragen?**
6 Please ______ with your talk.	Bitte **fahre** mit deinem Vortrag **fort**.

19 New words and phrases

▸ p. 135 | VOCABULARY p. 271

1	You can learn a lot about animals at the __________.	Im **Zoo** kann man viel über Tiere lernen.
2	Ella always ________________ her bike to school.	Ella **fährt** immer mit dem Fahrrad zur Schule.
3	What's the ______________________ of your talk?	Was ist das **Thema** deines Vortrags?

20 Word partners

Verbinde die Wörter und Ausdrücke, die zusammenpassen.

cycle   buy sth.   match   little   grandparents   kind   old

your parents' parents   game   friendly   not new   ride a bike   small   get sth.

21 Secret sentence

Ergänze die fehlenden Buchstaben. Welcher geheime Satz verbirgt sich in diesen Sätzen?

1 I like **cook**☐**ng**.
2 I don't live in a **pal**☐**ce**.
3 We often watch football matches at the **stadiu**☐.
4 Mum loves having ☐**isitors**.
5 The **w**☐**ather** isn't good today.
6 Can we go to the **ice** ☐**ink**?
7 Can we **bu**☐ some sweets, please?
8 Our dog never ☐**arks**.
9 There's a **yo**☐**th centre** near our house.
10 Put your **rubbi**☐**h** in the bin!
11 I often get books from the **librar**☐.

The secret sentence is: ____

22 Let's talk: Über den Wohnort und die Nachbarschaft sprechen

▸ p. 227

Beschreibe einer englischen Freundin oder einem englischen Freund deinen Wohnort und was es in der Nachbarschaft gibt oder nicht gibt. Vervollständige zunächst den Notizzettel mit eigenen Informationen. Du kannst deine Beschreibung auch aufnehmen und jemanden b tten, sie sich anzuhören und dir Feedback zu geben.

Where I live and what I can do there

★ I live in ____________________.

★ That's a big/small ____________ in ____________.

★ We live in a __________ / on an __________ / by __________ / in the ____________________.

★ My neighbourhood is ____________ / has ____________.

★ There is/are ____.

★ There isn't a /aren't any ____.

★ I (don't) like living here because ____.

23 Let's talk: Feedback geben

▸ p. 231

Ein/e Klassenkamerad/in hält eine Präsentation auf Englisch.
Welches Feedback kannst du ihm/ihr auf Englisch geben, während er/sie spricht?
Welches Feedback kannst du im Anschluss an die Präsentation a.uf Englisch geben?
Schreibe es auf die jeweilige Zeile.

1 Die Person spricht zu leise: ____________________

2 Die Person spricht zu schnell: ____________________

3 Die Person schaut euch nicht an: ____________________

4 Du fandest die Informationen nützlich: ____________________

5 Du fandest die Präsentation sehr schön: ____________________

6 Darum möchtest du der Person sagen, dass sie das toll gemacht hat:

____

Unit 5
Enjoy!

1 New words and phrases

▸ pp. 148–149 | VOCABULARY pp. 271–273

1	Sanya ______________ playing with her cat.	Sanya **genießt es**, mit ihrer Katze zu spielen.
2	Grandma makes great ______________.	Oma macht tolle **Nachspeisen**.
3	When's your ______________?	Wann hast du **Geburtstag**?
4	We always visit Grandma at ______________.	Wir besuchen zu **Weihnachten** immer Oma.
5	Tom likes ______________.	Tom mag **Obst**.
6	I love Grandma's red ______________.	Ich liebe Omas roten **Wackelpudding**.
7	In June we often have ______________ and ______________ for dessert.	Im Juni essen wir oft **Erdbeeren** mit **Sahne** zum Nachtisch.
8	Mick is ______________ lots of food.	Mick ist **gegen** viele Lebensmittel **allergisch**.
9	Raj works in an ______________.	Raj arbeitet in einem **indischen Restaurant**.
10	He knows lots of different ______________.	Er kennt viele verschiedene **Gerichte**.
11	Do you eat ______________?	Isst du **Fleisch**?
12	Sina is a ______________.	Sina ist **Vegetarierin**.
13	I take ______________ sandwiches to school.	Ich nehme **Käse**brote mit zur Schule.
14	There are green and yellow ______________.	Es gibt grüne und gelbe **Erbsen**.
15	We have ______________ in our garden.	Wir haben **Tomaten** in unserem Garten.
16	Raj uses lots of ______________ for his dishes.	Raj verwendet viele **Gewürze** für seine Gerichte.
17	We ______________ eat at home.	Wir essen **meistens** zu Hause.
18	Many British people eat white ______________.	Die meisten Britinnen und Briten essen Weiß**brot**.
19	______________ often comes from India or China.	**Reis** kommt oft aus Indien oder China.
20	Lara often eats meat and ______________.	Lara isst oft Fleisch mit **Gemüse**.
21	I need a ______________ for a vegetarian dish.	Ich brauche ein **Rezept** für ein vegetarisches Gericht.
22	Vegetables are good for your ______________.	Gemüse ist gut für deine **Gesundheit**.
23	Sina loves animals. ______________ she's a vegetarian.	Sina liebt Tiere. **Aus diesem Grund** ist sie Vegetarierin.
24	Lara's grandma is very ______________.	Laras Oma ist sehr **religiös**.

2 New words and phrases

▸ pp. 150–151 | VOCABULARY p. 273

1 Sam has an ________________ to Cara's party.	Sam hat eine **Einladung** zu Caras Party.
2 Lucy doesn't eat ________________.	Lucy isst keine **Würstchen**.
3 Jake loves ________________.	Jake liebt **Kuchen**.
4 Today is Dima's ________________.	Heute ist Dimas **zwölfter Geburtstag**.
5 He's going to the ________________.	Er geht in den **Zirkus**.
6 Don't text me but let me know ________________, please.	Schick mir keine SMS, sondern informiere mich **per Telefon**, bitte.
7 What's your favourite ________________?	Was ist deine liebste **Jahreszeit**?
8 What ________________ is Cara's party?	An welchem **Datum** ist Caras Party?
9 Sometimes people say or do funny things ________________.	Manchmal sagen oder tun die Leute lustige Dinge **am ersten April**.

3 Letter code

Welche Buchstaben sind 1, 2, 3 und 4?

1 C3n we g4 t4 3n 2nd23n re1t3ur3nt?
2 2'd l2ke 3 veget3r23n d21h.
3 21 th21 d21h very 1p2cy?
4 Wh3t'1 f4r de11ert t4d3y?

1:

2:

3:

4:

4 New words and phrases

▸ pp. 152–153 | VOCABULARY p. 273

1 I'm tired. I need to ________________.	Ich bin müde. Ich muss **mich ausruhen**.
2 Lucy can ________________ with four balls.	Lucy kann mit vier Bällen **jonglieren**.
3 Kim never ________________ before 9 p.m.	Kim **schläft** nie vor 21 Uhr.
4 John ____________ always do his homework before he can play with his friends.	John **muss** immer seine Hausaufgaben machen, bevor er mit seinen Freunden spielen darf.
5 Which subjects does Ms Black ____________?	Welche Fächer **unterrichtet** Frau Black?
6 Tom's cat often ________________ on his bed.	Toms Katze **liegt** oft auf seinem Bett.
7 Let's buy some ________________ for Cara.	Lasst uns ein paar **Ballons** für Cara kaufen.

5 Months

Schreibe auf, welcher Monat gesucht wird.

1 The fourth month ____________

2 The twelfth month ____________

3 The third month ____________

4 The tenth month ____________

5 The seventh month ____________

6 The second month ____________

7 The eighth month ____________

8 The first month ____________

9 The fifth month ____________

10 The ninth month ____________

11 The eleventh month ____________

12 The sixth month ____________

6 New words and phrases

▸ p. 154 | VOCABULARY p. 274

1	Tom always gets lots of ____________ for his birthday.	Tom bekommt immer viele **Geschenke** zum Geburtstag.
2	Next year he would like to have a ____________ ____________.	Nächstes Jahr möchte er einen **Zauberkasten**.
3	"Do you have an idea for a present for Molly?" – "____________ good book?"	„Hast du eine Idee für ein Geschenk für Molly?" **„Wie wäre es mit einem** guten Buch?"
4	"Are you ____________ that she likes reading?"	„Bist du **sicher**, dass sie gerne liest?"
5	I have to go home now. It's ____________ 6 o'clock.	Ich muss jetzt nach Hause gehen. Es ist **schon** 18 Uhr.

7 Nouns and adjectives

Sieh dir die Nomen in der Box an. Wandle sie in Adjektive um und vervollständige dann die Sätze damit.

Britain • cloud • fun • Germany • health • spice • sun

1 We usually eat ____________ food like fruit and vegetables.

2 My little brother doesn't like ____________ dishes.

3 On ____________ days I stay inside and read a book or draw a picture.

4 ____________ schools have a uniform, ____________ schools usually don't have a uniform.

5 My sister has lots of ____________ hats.

6 On ____________ days we often go to the beach.

8 New words and phrases

▸ pp. 155–156 | VOCABULARY pp. 274–275

Sieh dir die Lücken in den Sätzen und die Fotos an und löse das Kreuzworträtsel.

6

10

12

7

1 What ??? of food do you like?

2 Are there any strawberries in the fruit ??? ? I need to know because I'm allergic to them.

3 This cake is great. Can I have another ??? of it, please?

4 I'm writing a ??? of the things that I need to buy.

5 We need a ??? of white bread.

8 This cake is too sweet for me. There is too much ??? in it.

9 Can you see fish and chips on the ??? ?

11 You can make ??? from **no. 12**.

9 Listen carefully!

10

Zoe und Phil sprechen über Caras bevorstehende Geburtstagsparty. Höre ihnen aufmerksam zu und schreibe die fehlenden Wörter in die Lücken. Schreibe Zahlen als Wörter, nicht als Ziffern.

1 **Zoe:** Cara's birthday is on the ______________________ of ___________________.

2 **Phil:** Do you have an ________________________ to her ___________________?

3 **Zoe:** Yes, I do, but it's on _______________________. That's the ______________ of ________________.

4 **Phil:** That's right. Do you have an idea for a _______________ for her?

5 **Zoe:** Yes, I do. I want to __________ her a ticket for the __________.

6 **Phil:** That's __________! _____ ________ ______ get three tickets? Then we can go ____________________.

7 **Zoe:** ________ _______ _______. The tickets are quite ________________.

8 **Phil:** Okay. Do you have ______________ _______________?

9 **Zoe:** Cara likes _________________. Maybe you can get her some cool _______ ________.

10 **Phil:** Good idea! Thank you. _________ _________ __________.

10 Odd word out

Unterstreiche das Wort, das nicht in die Reihe passt.

1 tomato – dessert – pea – carrot
2 melon – lemon – salad – strawberry
3 January – March – June – Christmas
4 meat – sausage – rice – ham
5 (to) stand – (to) sit – (to) lie – (to) wear
6 allergic – jelly – healthy – vegetarian

11 Word search ↓ ↑ ← ↘

Finde neun Verben im Buchstabengitter und kreise sie ein. Vervollständige dann die Sätze mit sechs von ihnen. Achte dabei auf die richtige Form des Verbs.

E	T	S	E	R	D
N	E	L	T	R	N
J	A	E	I	A	A
O	C	E	S	E	T
Y	H	P	B	W	S
E	L	G	G	U	J

1 Sarah is ________________________ a nice piece of cake.
2 We have chairs. Why are you ________________ on the floor?
3 Philip can __________________________ with four balls.
4 The baby is tired. It's time to go to bed and ________________.
5 Does Mr Clark _______________________ English and PE?
6 Mick is ___________________________ a funny tie today.

12 New words and phrases

▸ p. 158 | VOCABULARY pp. 275–276

1	You only need 50 ________________ of sugar for this cake.	Du brauchst nur 50 **Gramm** Zucker für diesen Kuchen.
2	How much ________________ do we need?	Wie viel **Mehl** brauchen wir?
3	"Do we need water?" – "Yes, 100 ________________."	„Brauchen wir Wasser?" – „Ja, 100 **Milliliter**."
4	You need ____________ to make these muffins.	Zum Backen dieser Muffins benötigst du **Öl**.
5	Would you like some hot ________________?	Möchtest du heißen **Kakao**?
6	I always drink ____________ in the morning.	Ich trinke morgens immer **Milch**.
7	Be careful with the ________________!	Sei vorsichtig mit den **Eiern**!
8	Eating too much ____________ is unhealthy.	Zu viel **Salz** zu essen ist ungesund.
9	"How much sugar do you take?" – "One ________________, please."	„Wie viel Zucker nimmst du?" – „Einen **Teelöffel**, bitte."
10	My favourite ice cream is ________________.	Mein Lieblingseis ist **Vanille**.
11	Do we need ________________?	Brauchen wir **Backpulver**?
12	There's a lot of ____________ on this cake.	Auf diesem Kuchen ist viel **Glasur**.
13	Do you want ____________ on your sandwich?	Möchtest du **Butter** auf dein Sandwich?
14	Green is a ____________ of blue and yellow.	Grün ist eine **Mischung** aus blau und gelb.
15	You need an ____________ to bake a cake.	Du brauchst einen **Backofen**, um einen Kuchen zu backen.
16	Don't ________________ the picture.	**Zerbrich** das Bild nicht.
17	Let's ________________ Cara's birthday cake.	Lass uns Caras Geburtstagskuchen **dekorieren**.

13 Bits and pieces

Verbinde die Teile miteinander, um Wörter zu bilden.

1 milli | 2 saus | 3 dif | 4 tea | 5 van | 6 mix | 7 bal | 8 pres

illa | spoon | loon | ture | ent | litre | age | ference

14 New words and phrases

▸ p. 159 | VOCABULARY p. 276

1	What do you ______: cycling or walking to school?	Was **magst** du **lieber**: Radfahren oder zu Fuß zur Schule gehen?
2	I'm sorry, but this answer is ______.	Tut mir leid, aber diese Antwort ist **falsch**.
3	Is it ______ that you have a new job?	Ist es **wahr**, dass du einen neuen Job hast?
4	Let's ______ some vegetables for dinner.	Lass uns etwas Gemüse zum Abendessen **braten**.
5	Do you like ______ food?	Magst du **herzhaftes** Essen?
6	______	*das kleine runde Milchbrötchen, leicht süß, oft mit Rosinen* 
7	Can we sit at the ______ table over there?	Können wir uns an den **runden** Tisch dort drüben setzen?
8	Mum makes nice strawberry ______.	Mama macht gute Erdbeer**marmelade.**
9	We sometimes have ______ for lunch.	Wir essen manchmal **Hühnchen** zu Mittag.
10	This cake ______ very nice.	Dieser Kuchen **schmeckt** sehr gut.

15 New words and phrases

▸ p. 160 | VOCABULARY pp. 276–277

1	I'd like fish as a ______.	Ich möchte Fisch als **Hauptgericht**.
2	What ______ your brother ______?	Wie **heißt** dein Bruder?
3	______ is an African state. Many ______ speak English as a second language.	**Nigeria** ist ein afrikanischer Staat. Viele **Nigerianer/innen** sprechen Englisch als Zweitsprache.
4	You need ______ for lots of dishes.	Du brauchst für viele Gerichte **Zwiebeln**.
5	Sam likes red ______.	Sam mag rote **Paprika**.
6	Grandma bakes ______ cakes.	Oma backt **leckere** Kuchen.
7	______ are a healthy snack.	**Bananen** sind ein gesunder Snack.
8	Do you want sugar or ______?	Möchtest du Zucker oder **Honig**?
9	Homework is ______.	Hausaufgaben sind **wichtig**.
10	Christmas is part of our ______.	Weihnachten ist Teil unserer **Kultur**.
11	It's an old ______ to give presents to your family at Christmas.	Es ist eine alte **Tradition**, der Familie zu Weihnachten Geschenke zu machen.
12	My family likes ______ food. One day I would like to travel to ______.	Meine Familie mag **chinesisches** Essen. Ich möchte gerne einmal nach **China** reisen.

13 Let's make a ______ for dinner.	Lass uns etwas **kurz in der Pfanne Gebratenes** zum Abendessen machen.
14 In China, people eat ______ for breakfast.	In China essen die Leute **Nudeln** zum Frühstück.
15 Do you drink ______ or ______?	Trinkst du **Tee** oder **Kaffee**?

16 Lost words

Vervollständige die Sätze mit den Wörtern aus den Luftballons.

1 We need 400 grams __of__ flour for the cake.
2 Tess always wears nice things ______ her birthday.
3 Rishi is allergic ______ strawberries.
4 Christmas is ______ the 25th ______ December.
5 It's very cold ______ the moment.
6 Let's break ______ the chocolate and share it.
7 Dima has an invitation ______ Cara's party.
8 "I can't think of a present." – "What ______ a CD?"
9 What kind ______ music does Cara like?
10 Please buy two packets ______ bread.
11 What's ______ dessert?

17 New words and phrases

► p. 161 | VOCABULARY pp. 277–278

1 ______ is a small ______ between lunch and dinner.	Der **Nachmittagstee** ist eine kleine **Mahlzeit** zwischen Mittag- und Abendessen.
2 For some kinds of cake it is important to ______ the oven.	Bei einigen Kuchenarten ist es wichtig, den Ofen **vorzuheizen**.
3 He/She is ______ the ______.	Er/Sie **rollt** den **Teig aus**.
4 Would you like a ______ of water?	Möchtest du ein **Glas** Wasser?
5 I can ______ the fruit for the salad.	Ich kann das Obst für den Salat **schneiden**.
6 We usually eat rice or ______ for lunch.	Wir essen meistens Reis oder **Kartoffeln** zu Mittag.
7 Please clean the table. There are lots of ______ on it.	Bitte säubere den Tisch. Da sind viele **Krümel** darauf.
8 Use ______ for savoury dishes.	Verwende **Knoblauch** für herzhafte Gerichte.

18 New words and phrases

▶ pp. 162–163 | VOCABULARY p. 278

1	Look, the boy over there is ______________. Do you know him?	Guck mal, der Junge da drüben **winkt**. Kennst du ihn?
2	Jake's favourite subject is history. He ________ very ______________.	Jakes Lieblingsfach ist Geschichte. Er **ist** sehr **gut darin**.
3	Tim and his friends don't ______________ sit around. They often clean up the beach.	Tim und seine Freunde sitzen nicht **bloß** herum. Sie säubern oft den Strand.
4	Max speaks ______________ French.	Max spricht **ein wenig** Französisch.
5	______________________________.	**Mach dir keine Sorgen.**
6	I can't draw ______________.	Ich kann keine **Gesichter** zeichnen.
7	Lara always ______________ when you meet her.	Lara **lächelt** immer, wenn man sie trifft.
8	On Mondays ______________ Lara's ______________ to do the cooking.	Montags **ist** Lara mit Kochen **an der Reihe**.

19 Different sounds

Welcher Vokallaut klingt anders als die anderen in der Reihe? Unterstreiche das Wort. Suche dann zu jeder Zeile zwei passende Wörter im Kasten.

1 kind – I – line – big ______________________

2 wave – eight – have – late ______________________

3 just – glue – fun – club ______________________

4 no – go – how – know ______________________

5 tea – head – free – three ______________________

brave • come • hate • me • mice • nice • run • show • sweet • slow

20 New words and phrases

▶ p. 167 | VOCABULARY p. 279

1	Harry is ______________ his family history.	Harry **erforscht** seine Familiengeschichte.
2	Can we __________ some eggs for breakfast?	Können wir Eier zum Frühstück **kochen**?
3	Your text needs an ______________.	Dein Text benötigt eine **Einleitung**.
4	Please read the ______________ before using the magic set.	Bitte lies die **Anweisungen**, bevor du den Zauberkasten benutzt.

21 Listen carefully!

11

Höre dir die Sätze aufmerksam an und schreibe die fehlenden Wörter in die Lücken.

1 John works as a ____________ at an ____________ ____________.

2 He knows a lot of ____________ ____________.

3 He only cooks and eats ____________ ____________.

4 Luana loves ____________.

5 She always ____________ a ____________ ____________ for her mum.

6 She has a good ____________ ____________.

7 Harry doesn't cook or eat ____________ food.

8 He doesn't take ____________ or ____________ in his ____________.

9 Marnie only eats ____________ dishes. She never eats ____________ or uses ____________.

10 Logan loves different ____________ food and drinks a lot of ____________.

22 Singulars and plurals

Schreibe auf, wie viele Menschen, Tiere oder Dinge du auf den Bildern siehst.
Denke an die unterschiedliche Bildung des Plurals.

1 

one tomato

2 

____

3 

____

4 

____

5 

____

6 

____

7 

____

8 

____

9 

____

10 

____

11 

____

12 

____

23 Let's talk: Über den Tagesablauf sprechen, sich verabreden

▸ pp. 229–230

Sieh dir die Fragen unten an und beantworte sie. Du kannst deine Antworten auch aufnehmen und jemanden bitten, sie sich anzuhören und dir Feedback zu geben.

Was sagst du auf Englisch, wenn ...

1 ... du jemanden fragen möchtest, was er/sie normalerweise am Wochenende macht?

____

2 ... du jemanden fragen möchtest, was er/sie gerade tut?

____

3 ... du fragen möchtest, wo die Party stattfindet? ______________________________

4 ... du dich für die Einladung bedanken möchtest? ______________________________

5 ... jemand dir eine Nachricht schicken soll, ob er/sie zu deiner Party kommen kann, oder nicht?

____

24 Let's talk: Über Essen und Lebensmittel sprechen

▸ p. 231

Stell dir vor, ein/e neue/r Klassenkamerad/in lädt dich und deine Familie zu einer großen Feier ein. Ihr verständigt euch über eure Essgewohnheiten auf Englisch, da ihr/sein Deutsch noch nicht so gut ist. Du kannst deinen Text auch aufnehmen und jemanden bitten, ihn sich anzuhören und dir Feedback zu geben.

Sage, ...

- dass ihr viel Obst und Gemüse esst;
- dass ihr vegetarisches Essen mögt, da es gesund ist;
- dass deine Schwester Veganerin ist;
- dass deine Eltern Fleisch essen;
- dass du allergisch gegen Äpfel bist;
- was dein/euer Lieblingsessen ist.

Frage, was dein/e Klassenkamerad/in isst.

°Unit 6
The lost dog

1 New words and phrases

▸ pp. 182–183 | VOCABULARY pp. 279–280

1 Please buy a ________________ of milk.	Bitte kaufe eine **Flasche** Milch.
2 Sand and water make sea glass ____________.	Sand und Wasser machen Meerglas **glatt**.
3 Don't drink this water. It looks ____________.	Trink das Wasser nicht. Es sieht **trüb** aus.
4 Climbing the ________________ on British beaches is fun.	Auf den **Felsen** an britischen Stränden zu klettern macht Spaß.
5 There are ______________ cinemas in my town.	Es gibt **mehrere** Kinos in meiner Stadt.
6 Sam likes wearing ________________ shirts.	Sam trägt gern **bunte** Hemden.
7 Holly ________________ because she doesn't want to give the dog back.	Holly **weint**, weil sie den Hund nicht zurückgeben möchte.
8 ________________ Mia is very ill.	Die **arme** Mia ist sehr krank.
9 Are you the ________________ of this car?	Sind Sie der **Besitzer** dieses Autos?
10 ________________ that I have a good job.	**Ich bin froh**, dass ich einen guten Job habe.
11 Today Lara ________________ her sister from school.	Heute **holt** Lara ihre Schwester von der Schule **ab**.
12 Is that your ______________ on the pony?	Ist das Ihr **Kind** auf dem Pony?
13 How many ________________ do you have?	Wie viele **Kinder** haben Sie?
14 I ______________ you can come to the party.	Ich **hoffe**, dass du zur Party kommen kannst.
15 Sam often helps in an ________________.	Sam hilft oft im **Tierheim**.
16 If you like the book, you can ____________ it.	Wenn du das Buch magst, kannst du es **behalten**.
17 We're going to France for ____________ days.	Wir fahren für **ein paar** Tage nach Frankreich.
18 Please ________________. The baby is asleep.	Bitte **flüstert**. Das Baby schläft.
19 I know where the canteen is. Just ________________ me.	Ich weiß, wo die Mensa ist. **Folge** mir einfach.
20 It's mean to ________________ other people.	Es ist gemein, über andere Leute zu **lachen**.
21 My dog likes ________________ my hand.	Mein Hund **leckt** mir gern die Hand.
22 Where can I ________________ my shoes?	Wo kann ich meine Schuhe **lassen**?

2 New words and phrases

▸ p. 184 | VOCABULARY p. 280

1	Do you keep a ______________?	Führst du **Tagebuch**?
2	Sina's party ______________ great.	Sinas Party **war** großartig.
3	Lots of people ______________ to Sina's party.	Viele Leute **kamen** zu Sinas Party.
4	______________ the weather was really nice.	**Gestern** war das Wetter richtig schön.
5	We ______________ football in the garden.	Wir **haben** im Garten Fußball **gespielt**.
6	We ______________ lots of fun.	Wir **hatten** viel Spaß.
7	Mia can't go to school ______________. She is still ill.	Mia kann **morgen** nicht zur Schule gehen. Sie ist immer noch krank.
8	Don't ______________ your brother.	**Tritt** deinen Bruder nicht.
9	When my dog sees a rabbit, he always ______________ it but never gets it.	Wenn mein Hund ein Kaninchen sieht, **läuft** er ihm immer **hinterher**, bekommt es aber nie.
10	Why are you crying? ______________?	Warum weinst du? **Was ist los?**
11	Alfie ______________ lots of animals in the zoo.	Alfie **hat** viele Tiere im Zoo **gesehen**.
12	What are you ______________?	Was **suchst** du?

3 Bits and pieces

Verbinde die Teile miteinander, um Wörter zu bilden. Schreibe die Wörter auf.

1 bot | 2 fol | 3 whis | 4 colour | 5 col | 6 chil | 7 sev | 8 tomor

dren | row | lect | eral | low | tle | ful | per

1 ______________

2 ______________

3 ______________

4 ______________

5 ______________

6 ______________

7 ______________

8 ______________

4 New words and phrases

► pp. 185–187 | VOCABULARY pp. 280–281

1 I can see ____________ in your eyes. What's wrong?	Ich sehe **Tränen** in deinen Augen. Was ist los?
2 Lola always ____________ her little brother when she comes home from school.	Lola **küsst** ihren kleinen Bruder immer, wenn sie aus der Schule nach Hause kommt.
3 I can't hear the ____________ when I'm in the garden.	Ich kann die **Türklingel** nicht hören, wenn ich im Garten bin.
4 Hi, Sina! ____________.	Hallo, Sina! **Komm herein.**
5 My dog always ____________ his ____________ when he sees me.	Mein Hund **wedelt** immer mit dem **Schwanz**, wenn er mich sieht.
6 Mr Berry has four ____________.	Herr Berry hat vier **Enkelinnen**.
7 On our estate there are lots of children my ____________.	In unserer Wohnsiedlung sind viele Kinder in meinem **Alter**.
8 There are ____________ 15 girls in our girls' club.	In unserer Mädchengruppe sind **ungefähr** 15 Mädchen
9 Horses are very ____________ animals.	Pferde sind sehr **starke** Tiere.
10 Lara and her friends always ____________ when they meet.	Lara und ihre Freundinnen **umarmen sich** immer, wenn sie sich treffen.
11 John bakes ____________ cakes.	John backt **wunderbare** Kuchen.
12 Yesterday Mum ____________ me some money.	Mama **hat** mir gestern etwas Geld **gegeben**.
13 What are you doing ____________?	Was machst du **heute Abend**?

5 New words and phrases

► pp. 188–189 | VOCABULARY p. 281

1 Louis is quite ____________ for his age.	Louis ist ziemlich **groß** für sein Alter.
2 Mia has long ____________.	Mia hat lange **Haare**.
3 I never walk ____________ the park at night.	Ich gehe nachts nicht **durch** den Park.
4 Let's call the ____________.	Lass uns die **Polizei** rufen.
5 My mobile is too big for my trouser ____________.	Mein Handy ist zu groß für meine Hosen**tasche**.

6 When children start walking, they often ________________.	Wenn Kinder Laufen lernen, **fallen** sie oft **hin**.
7 We can ask the ________________ over there to tell us the way to the hospital.	Wir können die **Polizistin** dort drüben nach dem Weg zum Krankenhaus fragen.
8 Two ________________ gave a talk at our school yesterday.	Zwei **Polizistinnen** haben gestern einen Vortrag an unserer Schule gehalten.
9 Louis and John are on the other side of the road. Let's ________________ and say hello.	Louis und John sind auf der anderen Straßenseite. Lass uns **hinüberlaufen** und hallo sagen.
10 Mias's father is a ________________.	Johns Vater ist **Polizeibeamter**.
11 Mia wants to be a ________________ too.	Mia möchte auch **Polizeibeamtin** werden.
12 Take your hands ________________ your trouser pockets when you give a talk.	Nimm die Hände **aus** den Hosentaschen, wenn du einen Vortrag hältst.
13 Mia is happy. She ________________ a nice birthday present for her friend.	Mia ist glücklich. Sie **hat** ein schönes Geburtstagsgeschenk für ihren Freund **gefunden**.
14 Grandpa often tells us stories from the ________________.	Opa erzählt uns oft Geschichten aus der **Vergangenheit**.

6 Missing words

Vervollständige die Sätze mit dem richtigen Wort.

cry • hope • hug • keep • kick • leave

1 Grandma likes to __________ me.

2 Don't __________ anything in the car.

3 Our baby __________ a lot.

4 Don't __________ your ball into my window.

5 I __________ you're OK!

6 Can you __________ a secret?

7 Lost words

Füge das richtige Wort aus den Luftballons in die Sätze ein.

1 Is there someone ___at___ the door?

2 Can we buy a bottle __________ lemonade?

3 Run __________ your ball before the dog gets it.

4 What's wrong __________ Paul? He looks very sad.

5 I'm looking __________ my cat.

6 Be careful. People often fall __________ these steps.

7 Let's take the cheese __________ of the fridge.

8 Laughing __________ other people isn't nice.

9 Grandma and Grandpa came __________ see us yesterday.

8 Scrambled words

Die Buchstaben sind durcheinandergeraten. Schreibe die Wörter richtig auf.

1 There are VESERAL dogs in the IMAANL ELSHTER. ______
2 ILDRCHEN usually like ULLOCOURF clothes. ______
3 DASTYEERY two ENLICPOEWOM came to our school. ______
4 We're going to the REEATHT HTNITOG. ______
5 Susan's UGANERDGRDAHT is a LICPOE FIOFCER ______
6 The LPOICE are GOKLOIN for a lost dog. ______

9 Different sounds

Welcher Vokallaut in jeder Zeile klingt anders als die anderen? Unterstreiche das Wort. Finde dann zu jeder Zeile zwei passende Wörter im Reservoir.

block • eye • if • kiss • loud • mouse • new • room • sock • time

1 cloudy – out – through – now ______ ______
2 smooth – school – rude – brush ______ ______
3 rock – old – box – clock ______ ______
4 fish – cry – child – file ______ ______
5 kick – lick – kid – like ______ ______

10 Opposites

Finde die Gegenteile.

1 (to) stand up ◄► ______
2 into ◄► ______
3 a lot of ◄► ______
4 true ◄► ______
5 sweet food ◄► ______
6 terrible ◄► ______
7 sunny ◄► ______
8 (to) give away ◄► ______

11 Word search ↓ → ↗ ↙ ↑ ←

Finde sieben Verben im Infinitiv im Wortgitter und kreise sie ein. Vervollständige dann die Sätze mit der Vergangenheitsform der Verben, die du in dieser Unit gelernt hast.

P	F	I	N	D
L	S	E	E	G
A	X	M	I	E
Y	O	V	Y	B
C	E	V	A	H

Yesterday ...

1 ... the weather ____________________ horrible.

2 Grandpa and Grandma ____________________ to see us.

3 We ____________________ a great time together.

4 We ____________________ lots of games.

5 Grandma ____________________ me some money for a new blazer.

6 Grandma and Grandpa ____________________ my new bedroom.

7 I ____________________ my mobile under my bed.

12 Right or wrong?

Lies die Sätze und kreuze an, ob sie richtig oder falsch sind.

	Right	Wrong
1 "Wonderful" means "terrible".	☐	☐
2 Another word for "child" is "kid".	☐	☐
3 A granddaughter is your mother's daughter.	☐	☐
4 You can use the word "tall" for people and buildings.	☐	☐

Verbessere die falschen Sätze.

____

____

____

13 Secret sentence

Ergänze die fehlenden Buchstaben. Welcher geheime Satz verbirgt sich in diesen Sätzen?

1 I have two cousins. They're my **a** ☐ **e**.
2 They have black **hai** ☐ like me.
3 You can **l** ☐ **ave** your bike here.
4 We live in a very **t** ☐ **ll** building.
5 It's **abou** ☐ 22 metres high.
6 I love strawberry ☐ **am**.
7 My blazer has no **p** ☐ **ckets**.
8 We need a ☐ **ottle of milk**.
9 Who is the **o** ☐ **ner** of the black car?
10 **P** ☐ **or** Mandy is still ill.
11 Don't cycle in **st** ☐ **ong** winds.
12 A day at the beach is **won** ☐ **erful**.
13 Grandma **ca** ☐ **e** with us.
14 I'm so **gl** ☐ **d** that Grandma lives near us.
15 We ☐ **aw** lots of seagulls on the beach.
16 Grandma often tells funny stories from the **pas** ☐.
17 We found **a f** ☐ **w** pieces of sea glass on the beach.
18 I can write lots of interesting things in my **dia** ☐ **y** now.

The secret sentence is: ______________________________ !

Bye!

Have fun in the holidays

and see you soon

for Wordmaster 2!

ADVANCED
lighthouse 1

Wordmaster

Im Auftrag des Verlages erarbeitet von
Ursula Fleischhauer, Hannover

In Zusammenarbeit mit der Englischredaktion Klaus Unger (Projektleitung), Lisa Ahmadi sowie Elizabeth Pancake-Steeg und Chelsea Ledvinka-Heß

Lizenzmanagement
Silke Kirchhoff

Illustrationen
Evelt Yanait, Advocate Art
Scout-Illustrationen: Irina Zinner, Hamburg

Fotos
Anja Poehlmann, Brighton
Für die freundliche Unterstützung danken wir der Varndean School, Brighton

Umschlaggestaltung
Rosendahl, Berlin

Layoutkonzept
Klein & Halm, Berlin

Layout und technische Umsetzung
designcollective, Berlin

Druck
Livonia Print, Riga

PEFC zertifiziert
Dieses Produkt stammt aus nachhaltig bewirtschafteten Wäldern und kontrollierten Quellen.
www.pefc.de
PEFC/12-31-006

www.cornelsen.de

1. Auflage, 1. Druck 2023
978-3-06-034603-5

Quellenverzeichnis

Titelbild
Cornelsen/Personen: Anja Poehlmann,
Brighton Pier: mauritius images/Steve Vidler

Illustrationen
Cornelsen/**Adrian Barclay** (S. 1 Illustration des Buchumrisses); Cornelsen/ **Evelt Yanait** (S. 1 Max, S. 2, S. 3 un., S. 5, S. 7, S. 8/1–3, S. 9, S. 11, S. 13 , S. 17, S. 21, S. 22 un., S. 23, S. 25, S. 31, S. 32, S. 36, S. 53, S. 68, S. 77 ob., S. 84); **Irina Zinner** (S. 8/ob., S. 15, S. 20, S. 29, S. 30, S. 37, S. 55/Scout, S. 57, S. 62/Scout, S. 71, S. 80, S. 85, S. 87/Scout)

Abbildungen
S. 4: 1 stock.adobe.com/mdorottya, 2 stock.adobe.com/Cobalt, 3 stock.adobe.com/AVD, 4 Shutterstock.com/Charlie Edwards; **S. 6:** Fahrrad Shutterstock.com/stockphoto-graf, Roller stock.adobe.com/3dmavr; **S. 12:** London Shutterstock.com/S.Borisov; **S. 14:** Sian+Liam Shutterstock.com/Rido; **S. 15:** Baby Shutterstock.com/Vasiuk Iryna; **S. 18:** Ziege Shutterstock.com/Eric Isselee; **S. 19:** Fußball stock.adobe.com/Solid photos; **S. 22:** Hund stock.adobe.com/kisscsanad; **S. 26:** stock.adobe.com/Mircea Costina; **S. 27:** 1 stock.adobe.com/Wendy Devent, 2 Shutterstock.com/del-Mar, 3 Shutterstock.com/Konstantin Aksenov, 4 Montage: stock.adobe.com/Aleksandr_Villou, 5 Shutterstock.com/fizkes, 6 Shutterstock.com/baibaz, 7 Shutterstock.com/Africa Studio, 8 Shutterstock.com/Africa Studio, 9 Shutterstock.com/Yeamake, 10 Shutterstock.com/stuar, 11 Shutterstock.com/Bosnian, 12 Shutterstock.com/Dima Moroz, 13 stock.adobe.com/2ragon, 14 stock.adobe.com/Olga, 15 stock.adobe.com/Igor Savenchuk, 16 Shutterstock.com/rudolfgeiger, 17 stock.adobe.com/Aleksandr_Villou; **S. 28:** stock.adobe.com/Mila May; **S. 35:** ob. Shutterstock.com/margouillat photo, un. Shutterstock.com/Oksana Kuzmina; **S. 55:** Uhr Shutterstock.com/Stock2468; **S. 56:** stock.adobe.com/BillionPhotos.com; **S. 59:** stock.adobe.com/Joe Gough; **S. 60:** stock.adobe.com/william87; **S. 61:** Shutterstock.com/Chema.Velasco; **S. 62:** un. Shutterstock.com/Tim M; **S. 64:** li. Shutterstock.com/trofalenaRV, re. Shutterstock.com/StockLite; **S. 65:** ob. stock.adobe.com/hobrath, un. Shutterstock.com/venimo; **S. 70:** re. Shutterstock.com/Boule; **S. 73:** 6 Shutterstock.com/Gita Kulinitch Studio, 7 Shutterstock.com/Yellow Cat, 10 Shutterstock.com/Nattika, 12 Shutterstock.com/Bekshon; **S. 74:** Shutterstock.com/naulicrea; **S. 76:** Shutterstock.com/Steve Cordory; **S. 77:** un. Shutterstock.com/Yusak_P; **S. 79:** 1 stock.adobe.com/Olesia, 2 stock.adobe.com/Anatoliy Samara/2xSamara.com, 3 Cornelsen/bus: stock.adobe.com/Konstantinos Moraiti, 4 stock.adobe.com/#2464635/peopleimages.com, 5 stock.adobe.com/Rita Kochmarjova, 6 stock.adobe.com/absolutimages, 7 Shutterstock.com/Nosyrevy, 8 stock.adobe.com/grafikplusfoto, 9 stock.adobe.com/vadim kozlovsky, 10 stock.adobe.com/Trendsetter Images, 11 stock.adobe.com/m_a, 12 stock.adobe.com/Konstantinos Moraiti; **S. 81:** Shutterstock.com/Paul Nash; **S. 82:** Shutterstock.com/GoodStudio; **S. 83:** Pferde stock.adobe.com/HPE; Erdbeertorte Shutterstock.com/Semen Kuzmin, Schokotorte stock.adobe.com/studio.com (Olga Yastremska and Leonid Yastremskiy)/africa/Africa Studio; **S. 86:** Mi. Shutterstock.com/Ruslan Huzau; **S. 87:** Marmelade/ob. stock.adobe.com/alter_photo